"Benjamin Hedin went looking for the civil rights movement's past, but he also ran smack into the present, which can suddenly look like the past and then just as suddenly look totally different. By bringing stirring people like Septima Clark into focus, Hedin does what good historians do, but by entwining history with current events, he does a lot more. Here is a haunting meditation on living in history as well as with it."—Sean Wilentz, author of *The Rise of American Democracy: Jefferson to Lincoln*

"*In Search of the Movement* is a true marvel. Benjamin Hedin's insightful combination of reportage and history of the civil rights movement allows us to see the era with fresh eyes. By tracing the continued legacy of the black freedom struggle from the 1960s to the present, this gem of a book wonderfully illuminates how the movement is living and thriving in our own time." — Peniel Joseph, author of *Stokely: A Life* and *Waiting 'Til the Midnight Hour: A Narrative History of Black Power in America*

"Beloved community and the exuberant humanism of the civil rights movement have never been so vividly rendered. Carry this book with you as a guide through our own anxious age. Beautifully written, sharply observed, whimsical and tender, *In Search of the Movement* is a road trip into America's better self."—Charles Marsh, author of *God's Long Summer: Stories of Faith and Civil Rights*

"Fusing the personal with the political, the present with the past, Benjamin Hedin has written a sober, touching elegy for our shared history. *In Search of the Movement* is needed and essential, and it could not have come at a better time."—Saïd Sayrafiezadeh, author of *Brief Encounters with the Enemy* and *When Skateboards Will Be Free*

"A deeply intelligent writer and reporter, Benjamin Hedin repositions the civil rights movement as an ongoing crusade, a moral and political struggle that was seeded in the 1950s and 60s, but continues to develop in complicated, hopeful, and heartbreaking ways. *In Search of the Movement* is a bold and exploratory book, as much about Hedin's journey—to reconcile an American past with the American present—as anything else. It reads like both a salve and guide for these heady times; I couldn't put it down."
—Amanda Petrusich, author of *Do Not Sell at Any Price: The Wild, Obsessive Hunt for the World's Rarest 78rpm Records*

In Search

of the

MOVEMENT

In Search

of the

MOVEMENT

THE STRUGGLE FOR CIVIL RIGHTS THEN AND NOW

Benjamin Hedin

City Lights Books | San Francisco

Cover illustration (top): New York World-Telegram & Sun Newspaper Photograph
Collection. Reprinted by courtesy of Library of Congress, Prints & Photographs
Division.
Cover illustration (bottom): copyright © Sheilia Griffin. Reprinted by courtesy of
Sheila Griffin.
Cover design by Linda Ronan

Library of Congress Cataloging-in-Publication Data
on file

978-0-87286-647-8
eISBN: 978-0-87286-652-2

City Lights books are published at the City Lights Bookstore
261 Columbus Avenue, San Francisco, CA 94133
www.citylights.com

08 15

There must always be certain things that drop out of
history. Only the broadest movements and themes
can be recorded. All the multifarious choppings
and changings, all the individual hazards and
venturesomeness, and failures, cannot be recorded.
History is full of mysteries, even as family histories are
full of gaps and embellishments.

— V.S. Naipaul, *A Turn in the South*

From Chicago to New Orleans
From the muscle to the bone
From the shotgun shack to the Superdome
There ain't no help, the cavalry stayed home
There ain't no one hearing the bugle blowin'
We take care of our own
We take care of our own
Wherever this flag's flown
We take care of our own

— Bruce Springsteen, "We Take Care of Our Own"

If poetry is the little myth we make,
history is the big myth we live,
and in our living, constantly remake.

— Robert Penn Warren

CONTENTS

Preface

This book is, among other things, a record of conversation and encounter. Many of those I interviewed were elderly, and thus the burdens that life brings in the later decades became occupational routine. One woman who told me about the donation drives that supported the Montgomery Bus Boycott—about sending shoes to people who were now walking miles to work each morning and night—wouldn't let me photograph her because she didn't want to go through the chore of putting in her false teeth.

As many interviews as I did—and I kept to a rough goal of a hundred—I wish there had been more; chronicling the civil rights movement is one of the few activities that will make you long to be older. Watching Spike Lee's documentary *Four Little Girls*, about the Birmingham campaign of 1963, I say to myself: five or six more years. Had I been born that much earlier I might have interviewed figures like Fred Shuttlesworth and Wyatt T. Walker while they were still alive or still had some vitality about them. It's a fatuous wish, really, for I should be—and am—immensely grateful for the time I did spend in the company of men and women who marched in Birmingham and elsewhere. "The Moses generation," Barack Obama famously called them, and I share Garry Wills's belief that they are the rightful owners of the "greatest generation" mantle, normally bestowed on veterans of World War II.

The Moses generation dwindles in number each year, and soon it will belong entirely to memory. Some of the conversations

I pursued with the sense that I would be among the last to foray into this territory. And if nothing else, I thought, I could provide a place for those who have not yet spoken to go on the record, though there is another reason why *In Search of the Movement* relies so heavily on quotation.

Many imagine the movement to be a unified or singular thing; the name suggests as much, and so does the popular imagery, the footage of marchers holding hands and swaying together in song. Yet it has always contained passionate division. Basic questions of strategy and constituency are never easily settled, meaning that for the writer a choric or dialogic approach is best, whereby not one voice is featured but several, creating a sort of surround in which the reader can grasp, firsthand, the tensions and personalities that carry this collaboration forward. My thanks to all those who gave so generously of their time and offered their testimony.

Introduction

The American civil rights movement, I was always taught, was a moment in time, something that happened in the middle of the last century, went on for about a decade and a half, and then stopped. That's how many courses in high school and college treat it, and it's also how the movement is normally portrayed on television. First there was Rosa Parks's arrest in 1955 and a bus boycott in Montgomery, Alabama. Over the next decade, plenty of demonstrations were staged, some eliciting reprisals in the form of tear gas, dogs, and fire hoses. There was a march on the nation's Capitol, where Martin Luther King Jr. delivered his famous "I Have a Dream" speech; some important legislation was passed; and finally, in 1968, King was shot and it all petered out. Short form, that's the story. It has a clear beginning and a clear ending.

I never questioned this narrative, and while it is tempting to add, "despite having received a fair amount of education," it was my education, after all, the courses I had taken, the movies I watched, that had introduced me to and reinforced that story. It was all I knew. A few years ago, however, I met David Dennis, who had been one of the leaders of the Mississippi Summer Project of 1964, or Freedom Summer, as it is commonly known. I was then writing the outline for a documentary set during Freedom Summer, and reading books about that time, when hundreds of college-age volunteers, most of them white, traveled to Mississippi. In those days the state was regarded by many as the most intractable bastion of segregation. Its schools had not complied with the *Brown v. Board of Education* decision issued a decade earlier, and African Americans were prohibited, and often violently, from participating in elections. They didn't vote, and they didn't vote because they weren't allowed to register to vote. Civil rights leaders thought Mississippi would change only if the federal government intervened, and one way—perhaps the best way—of earning the government's attention was to bring in the volunteers, the sons and daughters of America's wealthiest and most influential families.

During my research I found out that David Dennis was now head of the Southern Initiative of the Algebra Project, a nonprofit created by Robert Moses, who had also helped coordinate Freedom Summer. Through a variety of programs, the Algebra Project tries to improve the education of students whose scores fall in the lowest-performing quartile on standardized tests, a demographic that is largely black and Hispanic. One place where they had established a residency was Summerton, South Carolina, in the same school district where *Briggs v. Elliott*, the first of the five cases combined in the *Brown* suit, originated. And that intrigued me, two former directors of Freedom Summer gathered at such a site. What were they doing, and what were their assessments of history? There had to be something there, I thought.

I wrote to David and his wife, Nancy, saying I would like to learn more about the work of the Southern Initiative of the Algebra Project, and possibly make it subject of a magazine story. Only they were not based in Summerton, as I had believed, but spending most of their time in Petersburg, Virginia. If you want to learn more, said David, come to Petersburg. I was slightly disappointed, for now, I concluded, the conceit of the story was lost, yet I nevertheless made plans to visit them in Virginia.

I need not have been disappointed—at least, not about the story. If I was looking for a link to the past, specifically the *Brown* case, I soon found that and much else. The public schools in Petersburg bore all the usual signs of failure. Accreditation was rare; the turnover of teachers and administrators was high. The district had a minimum of funding and no way to acquire more. Nearly all of the students I saw were African American, as most of the whites in the area attended private academies. The problem, in David and Nancy's eyes, was so vast that everyone had to be involved for a correction to occur, not only the parents, school board and teachers, but Petersburg's churches and businesses too. It was like the 1960s, Dennis said, when the vote was being lobbied for, and he would go from door to door, making new contacts and apprising them of their rights under law.

There were other similarities. Fifty years ago in Mississippi, he told me, "People wanted to vote, register; they wanted to participate in the structure of this country. The opposition was saying things like, 'Actually they don't want to register to vote.' They were getting someone from the plantation who said, 'No sir, I don't want to vote, I don't know what that's all about.' And this whole issue around education is so similar. The word is, these kids don't want to learn, these kids can't do this work, and we feel that we have to do something whereby the kids can actually have a voice to say, 'We do want to learn, we can do this work.'"

This comment convinced me to go and see Robert Moses and learn more about the Algebra Project's connection to the civil rights movement. The organization was started in 1982, the year Moses's eldest child, Maisha, entered middle school, and Moses noticed something troubling about her math classes. Generally the school's minority and poor students were being ushered out of the college track, and the education they received was, from one point of view, worthless, since it was hard to see it leading anywhere but to a service job. Moses designed the Algebra Project to counteract that trend, to find ways of giving students who might otherwise be written off the training they need to enter college and succeed when they get there. It's grueling work. Moses spends a lot of time in America's worst schools, encountering "sharecropper education," to use a phrase he coined. It means lackluster education, dead-end education, and evokes the sort of schooling that black Mississippi farmers—sharecroppers—received in the 1960s. Few of the schools were adequate. Classrooms were crowded and textbooks scarce, and older students could only attend for a handful of days, since they were needed in the fields. The system's purpose, insofar as it had one, was to ensure the preservation of an underclass.

There is one episode in particular Moses likes to recall from that time. In 1963 he was arrested while leading a voter registration drive in Greenwood, Mississippi. For black Mississippians, any attempt to register back then was mainly a symbolic gesture. The powers that be, the police or registrar, would close the courthouse office before your turn came, or, when you announced you wanted to register to vote, they would ask you to read and interpret a passage of the state constitution. At the hearing following his arrest, the judge asked Moses why he kept bringing illiterate sharecroppers down to the courthouse, where he knew a literacy test awaited that few of Greenwood's blacks could expect to pass. "We told him, in effect, the country couldn't have its cake and eat it too," Moses has written. "The nation couldn't deny a whole people access to education and literacy and then turn around and deny them access to politics because they were illiterate."

For this reason, Moses said, education was always "the subtext" to the quest for the vote. The two were inextricably tied, and once the ballot was gained, they would still be there, the legion of the uneducated, and sooner or later what was subtext would instead become central or primary.

"One way to think about the civil rights movement," I once heard him remark, "was that we got Jim Crow out of three distinct areas of the national life. We got it out of public accommodations;

we got it out of the right to vote." Here he was referring to two landmark pieces of legislation, the Civil Rights Act of 1964, which made segregation illegal, and the Voting Rights Act of 1965, which abolished literacy requirements and poll taxes and other loopholes formerly used to keep blacks out of the polling booth. I waited for the inevitable completion of the trinity, for him to say, "and we got it out of the schools" and to join those two bills with the *Brown v. Board of Education* decision. But that is not what he did. Instead he continued, "and we got it out of the national Democratic Party," and went on to describe the concluding act of Freedom Summer, when the movement brought its own political party to the 1964 Democratic National Convention in Atlantic City, New Jersey, and demanded that its delegates be seated on the convention floor. That demand was not met, but 1964 would be the last Democratic convention with an all-white delegation from the South.

"We did not get it out of education," Moses said. "That is the big unfinished job of the civil rights movement."

The more I talked with Moses and Dennis, the more my understanding of the civil rights movement began to change. Five decades ago they had been partners, teaming on the very difficult task of registering African Americans to vote in the Deep South, and they are still partners today, addressing the as yet unfinished job of securing equality in America's schools. Many days, they both remarked to me, their work feels the same now as it did then. I had always summoned the movement in grainy black and white, in the frames of old newsreels, but now I wondered if it truly was the province of the past and the past alone. Why did the form the civil rights movement took in the 1950s and 60s have to be the only possible one? And had I been conditioned to believe—as I think many whites have—that the struggle was finished with passage of legislation like the Civil Rights Acts of 1964, that the end of Jim Crow also meant the end of the movement?

I needed to speak with another member of the old guard,

to hear the views of someone else who had participated in those iconic campaigns of the 1960s. I reached out to Julian Bond, who had been director of communications for the Student Nonviolent Coordinating Committee, or SNCC, which was one of the most important civil rights groups of the time. Later Bond served as president of the NAACP, and, more to the point, he has been teaching the history of the civil rights movement for the past thirty years. If there was anyone who could help me understand the ways I was starting to question the standard account of things, it would be him. What do you tell your students? I asked.

"I say that it continues on and on," he answered. "I don't tell them that King got killed and it ended. When I began teaching and talked about the Montgomery Bus Boycott, the organization that ran it was still going, the Montgomery Improvement Association. The president was alive, and they still carried on activity. The movement is not something that happened way back then; I may start talking about it in a way-back-then period, but I tell them it's going on in the current time."

And if no ending can accurately be placed, the same can be said for the beginning, as there is no precise dawn of the civil rights movement. Any glance at history will show that the tensions and techniques that defined the 1950s and '60s were not new. Before there was a bus boycott in Montgomery in 1955, there was one in Baton Rouge in 1953; and before there was one in Baton Rouge in 1953, there was one in Harlem, in 1933. The Freedom Rides of 1961 were modeled on an earlier demonstration, one staged in 1947 and dubbed the Journey of Reconciliation. And read this:

> It appears that three negro men entered a Walnut street-car, going uptown, and refused to leave the same at the request of the driver. Acting under the positive rules of the company, the driver would proceed no further until the negroes left the car. This they refused to do, saying

that they had a right to ride in any public conveyance, and that the present was as good a time as any to test such rights of theirs. By this time a large crowd had gathered around the car, the negro element largely predominating, and threatening demonstrations were made against the driver and the whites in general . . .

This action on the part of these negroes bears every appearance of being a preconcerted attempt to test the right of the city railway corporations to forbid the riding of negroes or colored men on their cars.

Our instinct would be to date this passage to the 1960s, when such protests were routinely directed at white-only lunch counters and movie theaters and bus depots. Yet the above report was filed on October 31, 1870, in Louisville, Kentucky. Demonstrations similar to the one described occurred at the start of Reconstruction in New Orleans and Charleston as well. In all three cities African Americans won the right to ride on streetcars, and in Charleston, incidentally, the turning point came once an older black woman— Mary P. Bowers—refused to give up her place in the car and was rudely taken off. The story of her defiance is not so dissimilar, in the end, from that of Rosa Parks.

I am not trying to make a case for equivalence, and do not wish to convey the impression that I believe history to be the same across all eras. Examples of sit-ins can be found in Louisville in 1870 and in Charleston in 1867—and at other times too, such as in Washington, D.C., in 1943—but that does not mean they happened on the same scale or had the same effect as those that went on in the sixties. I am only saying it might be better to view the civil rights movement as a continuum, as a very long tradition, as opposed to a brief rupture. With that perspective, there would be periods of greater relative glory and periods of greater numbers, greater involvement; after all, it's no coincidence the word "movement" entered the popular lexicon in the 1960s and not before. But creation myths that say it sprang up, willy-nilly, on the Monday the Supreme Court announced its decision in the *Brown vs. Board of Education* case or on the Thursday Rosa Parks was arrested are not supported by the historical record. That type of history tells us more about certain needs that reside in the human brain—like the need for order, for narrative division and logic—than anything else.

And if the movement is a continuum, then in keeping with the meaning of that word, which connotes stability and permanence, a continuation of something, then quite possibly it never went away, not altogether. It could be out there even now, in some form. That was the implication of Julian Bond's comment, after all. So I decided to go looking for it. I wanted to find the civil rights movement in its contemporary guise, and that would also mean answering the critical question of what happened to it after the 1960s, after the "ending" of King's assassination.

———

With a project like this certain questions immediately come to mind. What do you mean by "civil rights movement"? is one. Large scale, my answer would be that it is any effort that strives to close the distance between America's rhetoric and its reality. The idea of America is loaded with promissory language, with phrases like "all men are created equal," and where those assurances give out—where circumstances force you to consider whether they are nothing but an abstraction, appealing but ultimately hollow—is where the search begins. Making America own up to itself: that, in the plainest terms, has always been the job of the civil rights movement.

Certainly, the meaning of the phrase "civil rights movement" has broadened over time, and today would include the efforts of undocumented immigrants, gays, and others to earn equal rights and equal treatment under the law. In this book, the term refers to the black freedom struggle, to a history of African American activity—of civil disobedience and community organizing—that is at least as old as our nation itself. In searching for evidence of the continued vitality of such a tradition, I have had to combine history with reportage and create a text that is Janus-faced, so to speak, looking simultaneously forward and back.

The book is structured to reflect my experience of that search, and focuses in particular on three intersecting issues: the push for fair and equal access to the vote, education, and health care. The first two, you might say, are staples of citizenship, but the third, does that qualify as a "civil right"? Voting clearly does, and people might begrudgingly count education as a right, if only out of a native fondness for children—but health care is the most controversial issue of our day, and even my most sympathetic readers might not allow that it belongs in the company of the other two. Over the years it has not earned the same kind of attention from historians and activists. To take it up, then, and include it here is to pace the outer limits of the civil rights movement and get a feel for its dimensions.

Next question: That's great, to go out and look for the movement, but how do you know when you've found it?

It would be easy to squirm out of that by saying the movement is irreducible, impossible to describe in its last detail, although when you've found it, well, you know you've found it. Alternately, I could cite numbers and attempt a strict quantification, but that leads to absurdity. If a march of 1,000 counts as a movement activity but only 999 show up, what is it then? Adjust your scale and all you do is invite more convolution. So on weeknights, and in communities with a population of under 20,000 . . . no, you just can't do it that way.

The essential quality to look for, in my opinion, is one I've

already hinted at: the sense of tradition, of being consciously in-
debted to the work of your predecessors. And if that sounds like
a sighing, middle-aged writer's view of things, I'd point to this:
After George Zimmerman was acquitted of the murder of Trayvon Martin, a group of students calling themselves the Dream Defenders, in homage to Martin Luther King's "I Have a Dream"
speech, commenced a sit-in at the governor's office in Florida.
The gesture was supported by the weight of historical precedent.
You might even say history told them to do it, and that's my point
about the movement's lineal character: often it is what suggests
the course of action. Another example would be Moral Monday, a
series of protests that began in the spring of 2013 in Raleigh, North
Carolina, after Republicans, who in the most recent elections had
assumed control of both the governorship and state legislature, en-
acted a string of controversial laws. Moral Monday is modeled on
the demonstrations that unfolded in Birmingham and Selma in the
1960s. William Barber, the leader of Moral Monday, even likes to
say "Raleigh is our Selma," and if you think for a moment of all the
movement is up against—prejudice's many forms, which may be
harder to combat as they become more covert than in eras past—
then you understand the need for a touchstone and a set of proven
tactics. Size up the movement this way, as a repertoire of techniques, and you not only liberate it from the hold of time; you get
a more accurate representation to boot. Robert Moses is occasionally called the father of the voting rights movement in America.
But when he left New York to begin working in Mississippi, Ella
Baker, a stalwart of the NAACP and other groups, whose experience stretched back to the Depression, said to him: remember, you
are continuing something, not starting it.

I also think it's fair to watch for results. The movement can be
found where things are being changed. All of those whose stories
appear in this book have exerted some appreciable influence, and
for those who believe that to be a cruel or utilitarian rubric, know

that the subject of how redeeming or valuable the struggle itself is will be taken up in the final chapter.

———

How do you know when you've found it? The question is in some ways more interesting than the answer. To find something you must know what you're looking for, and what's the most prevalent definition of the freedom struggle? The history of the movement is everywhere these days, since it's anniversary season: in 2011 the Freedom Rides turned 50; two years later it was the March on Washington, then Freedom Summer, and in 2015, the march from Selma to Montgomery. These dates have ensured the movement receives the full treatment of America's culture machine, and is spared none of its habitual embarrassments. Birmingham may always be known as the city where fire hoses were turned on black children, but that doesn't mean we should issue mugs commemorating the occasion, and special edition Coke bottles, though I can now walk into the gift shop at the Birmingham airport and buy both. I can also turn on the television, find a movement doc on practically any network, and watch the familiar train of images go by: the COLORED sign over the restroom, the placards that say FREEDOM NOW, King raising his hand at one pulpit or another, and the Klansmen riding around in a car with a cross on top, lit up garishly like some Christmas tree.

A peculiar thing happens to memory when that litany of photographs gets shown. A hardening takes place, as the inevitable effect of being exposed to the same version of history over and over is to narrow the movement down to its most public or visible manifestation, to marches, sit-ins, and the like. As a result, I'm not sure the civil rights movement in the popular mind means much more than a group of black people going out into the street with a sign and singing "We Shall Overcome." Eventually, the whites will show up with their baseball bats. It's a powerful scene, one that occurred plenty of times, but the movement does not always assume such a grandiose and cinematic shape. You can also find it in quieter, more everyday locales, in the back of a cooperative store, for instance, or a church basement. What happens there may not invite the television cameras, but one of the major lessons of this history is that there is not necessarily a correlation between fame—or visibility—and impact, and just as often you'll find the opposite, the largest footprint belonging to the unheralded. For this reason the book's title suggests another kind of search, and that is an attempt to understand the movement better, to rescue it from cliché and reclaim some wider meaning of the word.

Most of *In Search of the Movement* is set in the South, and I am half apologetic about that, but only half. Now as before, the South is where resistance to the freedom movement consolidates; it's where most of the new voter identification laws are being passed, where the Medicaid expansion is blocked, and so on. Time passes slowly in the South, people like to say.

Robert Moses had talked of subtexts lurking beneath old problems, and there are subtexts—but there are also old problems, and America has shown a talent of late for making the old into the new. The climate of our politics is astonishingly retrograde, shot through with talk of states' rights and the division between North and South, red and blue. Open the paper and it's yesterday's news—literally. One morning in 2014 the *New York Times* featured an item titled DESEGREGATION DEAL COMPLETED. The article described the court battles that had gone on in Little Rock, Arkansas, since 1957, when the city's Central High School admitted its first black students amid a backdrop of rioting and an occupation of troops from the 101st Airborne. In the intervening decades, Little Rock's public schools had mostly reverted to being all black or all white. The next day, in the same space of the front page, the headline ran FEDERAL SCRUTINY OF VOTING. This story focused on a small town in Alabama where in recent years African Americans had been denied access to the polls.

Ralph Ellison once stated that American history had a habit of "returning at a later point in time to an earlier point in historical space," and this was one of the moments when you could feel the pivot. The present is an open canvas: that is one of our most tenacious assumptions, yet reading about segregation in schools and modern-day interference with the ballot, I couldn't help but wonder if everything had been decided for us years ago, and we were all just going along for the ride. Finally, then, I decided to look for the movement because I thought whatever I found would help address that essential and vexing question: how much do we determine history, and how much are we determined by it?

PART ONE

Starting Points

I.

In 1871 the state of Georgia passed a statute that made sedition a capital crime, punishable by execution. The law was seldom enforced, though it was invoked in the trial of Angelo Herndon, a communist organizer arrested in Atlanta in 1932. Five years later, the Supreme Court overturned Herndon's conviction, ruling by a 5-4 margin the statute was unconstitutional, and the law again faded from use until August 1963, when three young men were arrested in Americus, Georgia. They had committed sedition, in the prosecutor's eyes, by encouraging African Americans to march against segregation. Since treason was a capital offense they were ineligible for bond, and when apprised of the case, Attorney General Robert Kennedy refused to challenge the indictment, so there would be no rescue courtesy of the federal government. The three were sent to jail wondering if they would end up in the electric chair.

Two of the prisoners, Ralph Allen and John Perdew, were white. They shared a cell six feet wide and ten feet long, while Don Harris, an African American, was assigned to the cell where black inmates were kept. Harris and Allen were veterans of the civil rights movement; they had been working in Georgia for the Student Nonviolent Coordinating Committee (SNCC) since 1961, but Perdew was a summer volunteer, a student at Harvard. A week after their incarceration, police in Americus arrested Zev Aelony, an older activist who had participated in the Freedom Rides of

1961. He too was charged with sedition. Soon they all became known as "the Americus Four."

Today Perdew lives along the south rim of Atlanta. On a recent trip to the city I called to let him know I was passing through, though when I knocked on his door at the appointed hour, he was not there. Instead, it was answered by a young man, a grandson of Perdew's, I thought, until I told him I was writing a book about the civil rights movement. "Oh, did he have something to do with that?" he asked.

A few minutes later Perdew and his wife came home, weary from a school board meeting. Perdew is from Denver, but his wife is Southern and possesses the Southerner's ability to absorb her fatigue into a ritualized politeness. After our greeting she started preparing dinner, and the young man I met at the door sat down at the table. His name was Markeys, I would learn later, and I would learn, further, that his mother worked as a prostitute and his father is in jail for life. The Perdews are his de facto guardians, though at that moment I did not know any of that, and simply saw someone of fifteen or sixteen arrayed in a tank top and jeans, who over the course of the next hour did not look up once from his phone, as Perdew and I began to talk about his arrest in Americus and its aftermath.

Nineteen sixty-three was an important and tumultuous summer, though if our subject is the sixties, then I guess that isn't too grand a claim, for they were all like that; the decade was one climacteric stretching into the next. What Perdew was caught up in, and became a footnote to, was segregation's last stand. In May 1963, Birmingham leaders relented to the pressure of a massive campaign that was taking place there and removed the white-only signs from department stores and diners, and in June the president sent a bill to Congress that, if passed, would forbid segregation across the board in all of America's public accommodations. At Harvard, Perdew knew someone who had been arrested in

Maryland for demonstrating with SNCC and described his experience in heroic language, and between that and the newspaper coverage of what was going on in Birmingham, Perdew was moved to write to SNCC and ask about work for the summer. He was assigned to Albany, Georgia, and arrested within a week of his arrival. After his release he was sent to Americus, forty miles north of Albany, in Sumter County. SNCC had been signing up black voters in Americus since the spring and organizing sit-ins to press for integration of the town's movie theater and other businesses. On the night of August 8, 1963, a mass meeting was held in Friendship Baptist Church.

"The church was packed," Perdew recalled, "and it was rocking. The freedom songs, the testimonies. When we left we found ourselves surrounded by sheriff's deputies and police and some state troopers. Some of them were armed with baseball bat–size billy clubs. And they waded into the crowd. I saw some attacking Don Harris; they picked him out and started beating him. I was at that point across the street, and before I knew it the city marshal was rushing at me, swinging a blackjack."

Police were outnumbered eight to one to begin with, and by this time the scene had drawn a large crowd. As Perdew was chased down, Harris was being buzzed with a cattle prod, and some of the onlookers began lobbing bricks and bottles at the officers, who in turn started using those billy clubs and firing shots overhead. Later the three affiliated with SNCC were booked on insurrection, unlawful assembly, and rioting. Except for sedition, that was standard protocol in the South at the time. Countless demonstrators had been jailed for the same offenses. To tack on insurrection was a desperate ploy, a last-ditch effort by the white politburo in Americus to discourage the movement and avoid another Birmingham. The strategy was borne out in the short run, as can be seen by the *New York Times* headline that led off coverage of the affair: STRICT LAW ENFORCEMENT STIFLES NEGROES' DRIVE IN AMERICUS, GA.

During his time in jail, Perdew was struck by fear at what might await him, not just the electric chair but perhaps a random beating or two, administered by the lawmen or one of the other prisoners, in case he ever changed cells. That never happened, and in the end his greatest foe was boredom. He and Allen were let out of their cell only once, and they had nothing to read except the occasional newspaper or magazine given to them by a jail trustee. Letters were delivered already opened, and long before federal judges overturned the sedition charge on November 1, 1963, Perdew had decided he would not return to Harvard.

"With three months to think about things, in that setting, you get pretty radicalized," he told me. "I decided to stay, not just because I missed registration. I felt like it was my fight. I had become a missionary—I very deeply believed in the need to resist this evil.

"Now, you've probably run into the argument advanced by some academics"—he stuck on the word, showing his dislike— "that the Albany movement was a failure. To me, that is the most ludicrous theory; it would be like calling Lincoln a failure because the Union lost a good bit of battles in the beginning of the Civil War. Our objective was building a resistance, building a movement of people who were ready and willing to stand up and defy Jim Crow. Any demonstration was in itself a victory."

It's true that the campaign in southwest Georgia is not looked upon favorably by historians. Although it was the focus of the movement in 1962, Albany is not a sacred word, does not stir up the triumphalist feelings that cities like Montgomery, Birmingham, and Selma do. There is a lack of benchmarks, and historians need those. What occurred in Albany cannot be tied to any legislation that passed through Congress, and there were no sudden changes to city ordinances. What promises the town leaders made about integration were insincere and left unfulfilled. Albany also failed to spawn an emblem, some image to lodge in the popular mind like Birmingham and its attack dogs. But does that make it a failure? Perdew, I felt, was right in pushing for a broader metric and urging that we take the long view. How to rate the activity of a repressed yet passionate people: history quails before the question, which would seem to lie outside binary categories like success and failure, and to call for a more complicated system of measurement.

While we were on the subject, I asked Perdew what else bothered him about movement histories. He answered, "I wish there was more about the day-to-day activity involved in building a movement—day-to-day, unglamorous activity. And I wish that people who write about the movement would be more helpful in building another movement. We need a movement. We're nowhere."

I paused, offering the silence as opportunity to issue a retraction. It was one thing for somebody of my generation to make this claim, someone in their thirties or forties, whose life postdated the sea changes of the 1960s. Then it would be a forgivable slip, a case of dinner party bravado or nearsightedness. But this was not a man of my generation. He had been threatened with execution for believing blacks and whites should eat in the same diner or swim laps in the same pool. In 1964, when Perdew married an African American—that was his first marriage—he had to go home to his native Colorado to do it, as interracial unions were illegal in Georgia. There was no one less likely, in my opinion, to say that we as a nation were nowhere, so I waited for the inevitable retreat, a turn toward, "Well, we've come a long way" or "I guess there are problems, though on the other hand . . ." but none of that came. He just looked at me, as if to make sure the comment had properly registered, and finally I said, "Would you really go so far as that, as to say we're nowhere?"

"There are more problems now than there were fifty years ago," he said. "And what we're fighting is more subtle."

Segregation, Perdew said, possessed a virtue concealed at the time, a virtue, like some tragic flaw, that was inseparable from what was most hideous about the institution: its omnipresence.

Segregation was everywhere, haunting every interaction, and whatever else it did, it gave the movement a clear target. "The enemy was so much more blatant," Perdew said. "I saw in the courthouse in Albany the two drinking fountains. The white-only, refrigerated unit and five feet away a cruddy old bowl, colored-only. What could more dramatically illustrate racism? Now it's more subtle and systematic and harder to fight." Even the sedition charge, he believed, had been a boon to the cause, the South's draconian absurdism serving to rally support. "Students charged with the death penalty," he said. "What could be more dramatic and helpful to organizing a movement?"

We talked for another hour, and then I left for my rental car. Outside Markeys was waiting in the shadows. He wanted to thank me, he said, though for what he didn't say and maybe couldn't say. For enlarging his sense of the man who was helping him was my guess—it was plain, cell phone aside, that he had been listening the whole time.

My destination that night was Montgomery, Alabama, a city widely viewed as the birthplace of the modern civil rights movement, and as I drove I reviewed Perdew's claim in my head, weighed the evidence on either side, for and against. And to do that was to enter a dizzying territory, a realm of competing facts where every thought immediately gave rise to and countenanced its opposite. "We need a movement," he had said. "We're nowhere." It was all too easy to agree with the second half of the assertion—and all too easy to rebut it.

———

When you write about the movement (as with anything else), there are little problems that assert themselves, and big problems. Everyone knows too much or not enough: that's one of the little problems. Civil rights is an academic cottage industry, and sometimes you interview a member of the freedom struggle who just got off the phone with a filmmaker or a German doctoral student. Their script is ready, the furrow is ploughed, and to eke out some novel observation from your talk seems a superhuman task. Meanwhile, your audience knows next to nothing, since the movement for most looms as a series of protests aimed at doing away with Jim Crow and nothing more. The writer, then, finds himself in no-man's land, trying to appeal equally to the spheres of expertise and ignorance.

That's one of the small problems, but the biggest concern by far is how little can be stated with perfect confidence. Everything you say must sooner or later be qualified, and Perdew's comment called to mind diplopia, the problem of doubleness, where two visions overlie one another, creating a blurry canvas. America looks the same out of each eye, although through one lens everything has changed and through the other nothing has. For an example we need only look at the moment most often identified as a turning point: the *Brown v. Board of Education* decision. It was supposed to do away with separate and unequal schools, but how many schools, in 2015, are actually integrated, boasting a healthy mix of races, and how many predominantly black school districts have as much money as the nearest predominantly white one? And yet the moment you start feeling fatalistic and have decided that race is an intractable dilemma, you can turn on the television, look at Barack Obama, and say no, something fundamental had to change in order for a black man to be elected president. But then—and there is always, in these internal dialogues, a *but then*—you think of what the election of Obama has engendered, the partisan politics, motivated, it often seems, by a deep current of racism, one that has managed to withstand the march of fifty years.

There seems but one way out of the infinite circle, and that is to take a view from up high of the span that must be traveled. For only in a colossally long race—an ultra marathon—can you have covered a long distance and still be nowhere near the finishing line. But that's not right, because the distance covered must be covered again—and again. Think of voting rights and education, the battles that are continually being revisited or restaged. Our history is not a linear or point-to-point progression; it does not consist entirely of forward movement but switches back every so often, and by the time I reached Montgomery, where the route to my hotel took me past the Alabama state capitol, its alabaster dome lit starkly and glowing with a lunar brilliance, I began to feel there was no way to resolve the contradictions.

————

"We need a movement," Perdew insisted, and yet these things are not easily started. In fact, they seem beyond purpose and planning, for if it were a question of will alone then the movement would have been willed into existence a hundred times over. There is no blueprint, not even in hindsight, and it's impossible to establish the lineage of cause-and-effect with absolute certainty. Place two events side by side and they can easily be shown to have a causal relationship; but the present is a delicate assemblage, and experience tells us the same set of circumstances might easily lead to different results. Surely there is some catalyst, a spark that gets us to where we are in lieu of the other possibilities, but we cannot tease it out, not verifiably. All we can say for sure, as we turn to some of the great beginnings in movement history, is that accident was essential, that in many cases a lot depended on the element of the unforeseen.

In itself, the bus boycott that occurred in Montgomery in 1956 was no accident. Certainly, the moment widely presumed to be unscripted was not. Rosa Parks's story is the stuff of folklore now. She was a tired woman, says the legend, who needed some rest on the ride home and decided to take a stand. Anybody can take a stand: that is the lesson of this particular fable. But Rosa Parks wasn't anybody. She had worked for the NAACP and attended workshops on desegregation the summer before, in July of 1955. "Desegregation," one note from these sessions reads, "proves itself by being put in action not changing attitude." Other women had been arrested on Montgomery's buses for violating the segregation ordinance. But Parks was the ideal resistor, a middle-aged woman with no blemishes in her background. On the night she was charged, E.D. Nixon, who had served for many years as president of Montgomery's NAACP chapter, said, "Mrs. Parks, this is the case we've been waiting for. We can break this situation on the bus with your case."

Nixon and his allies believed they could win a fight in the courts. Meanwhile, word of the boycott was distributed by the Women's Political Council, an outfit run by Jo Ann Robinson, a professor at Alabama State University. Depriving city buses of black patronage had been on her mind as early as 1954. Montgomery, in other words, was blessed with savvy local leadership, and the overall plan had already been devised. Where the situation becomes uncanny is with the arrival of Martin Luther King Jr. Nobody, neither Nixon nor Robinson nor anyone else, knew how powerful a presence was in town, living just up the hill. King's annunciation can be tracked to a single night, Monday, December 5, 1955. That afternoon he was appointed president of the fledgling Montgomery Improvement Association. The bus boycott had already begun, but as a test case, a one-day trial. A meeting occurred that evening at Holt Street Baptist Church to determine if it would continue through Tuesday and beyond, and after King spoke, there was no longer any doubt.

When King stepped to the pulpit he had only a few notes to guide his remarks. It was his first major speech as the leader of anything other than his own congregation, and what makes the oration memorable is the way he wrests every conceivable moral authority over to the side of desegregation. "If we are wrong," he says at one point, "then the Supreme Court of this nation is wrong. If we are wrong, the Constitution of the United States is wrong. If we are wrong, God Almighty is wrong." Now the movement had its leader, is how reports of this night customarily get written, but that's not quite right. Because it was more than that. Now the movement had a leader who was capable of infusing it with that distinctly American breed of philosophy: manifest destiny.

We find a similar pattern when we turn to the creation of SNCC, an organization founded in the wake of the sit-in movement. That began in Greensboro, North Carolina, on February 1, 1960, when four black college students sat at the counter in Woolworth's and asked to be served, even though it was against the law for them to eat there. Actually, the sit-ins had already started in Nashville, where workshops in the nonviolent techniques practiced by Gandhi had been going on for years, led by James Lawson, a Methodist preacher and pacifist. His classes, held in a church near Fisk University, were attended by the likes of Diane Nash, John Lewis, Bernard Lafayette, and James Bevel—a hall-of-fame roster if ever there was one.* In November 1959 Lawson and his acolytes staged a practice sit-in, and once the Christmas holiday was over, they planned to demonstrate on a massive scale. But they were preempted when the very thing they had been preparing for happened in Greensboro, one state over. On February 2, those four students returned to Woolworth's and were joined by nineteen others. On February 3 the number was closer to ninety, and sit-ins had begun in Raleigh and Durham. Over the coming weeks they would spread to other cities in the South, enlisting thousands,

---

* These four would have a hand in much of the movement's history in the 1960s. Lewis served as chair of SNCC from 1963 to '66; Lafayette was SNCC's first organizer in Selma, Alabama, and set the foundation for the voting rights struggle that would crest there in the spring of 1965. And Nash and Bevel, who were married for a time, were the ones responsible for the idea of marching from Selma to Montgomery.

many of whom would be on hand for the charter meeting of SNCC in April, held at Raleigh's Shaw University.

You could say the sit-in movement would have occurred anyway, originating out of Nashville as opposed to Greensboro. You can just as well say that Lawson and the others could have won desegregation in Nashville but without capturing the attention of the nation at large. All we have finally is the historical record, and in both cases—in Montgomery as well as Greensboro—the existing infrastructure was energized by some agency that lay outside the plan. Providence was a critical factor. Not the only factor, but historical memory, being what it is, tends to leave the planning and infrastructure behind, and everything gets subsumed into the legend of a single moment. I remember a remark made by Maisha Moses, the daughter of Robert Moses.* Maisha and I are roughly the same age; she organizes youth in urban schools, and we approach the events of the 1960s with what I think is an approximate amount of awe. Growing up, she spent a lot of time at SNCC reunions, and eventually realized that many of her elders hung on to the same question she did: how does this all get started in the first place?

"I think it was Chuck McDew," she said, mentioning the one-time chairman of SNCC. "He would say, 'Damn, I wish we knew how to start a movement.' After hearing them say this a few times it struck me, Well, if they don't know how to do it, then who does? I think it's something that's just so much bigger than any of us who are in it or try to be part of it. A river has a life of its own, and I think a movement is like that."

I asked her to clarify the metaphor, and she said, "A river has shape, boundaries, patterns of movement. But there's also unpredictability; scientists, there's a lot they can describe about water,

<hr />

* A native of New York City, Moses was the first member of SNCC to work full time on voter registration in Mississippi; he moved to the state in 1961. See pp. 141–170.

but they can't say that this water molecule that is now here is going to be over here after some given period of time. It's similar when people say they're starting a movement. What they're trying to do is catalyze an uprising. Nobody knows how to do that. Moments of uprising—those moments happen because they stand on years and years and years of work and organizing, and most of it hidden and some of it connected and some of it totally unconnected but somehow all contributing to this moment happening. And who can predict that?"

It does not happen instantaneously, in other words, even though that is how the story gets passed down. Only the most dramatic bits, the arrest of Rosa Parks, the students going to Woolworth's at closing time, make it through the sieve of history. Those moments, Maisha was saying, are catalytic, but no more essential than the planning and organizing that preceded them, even if our view of events tends to privilege one and overlook the other. Jo Ann Robinson, E.D. Nixon, James Lawson: they had no idea the galvanizing moment was up ahead and around the bend, and history makes the work they did seem like a faith act, something carried out in preparation for that moment—even though it wasn't. They were going to do it anyway.

2.

"Have you been following what's happening in North Carolina, with the NAACP leading a series of protests at the state capitol, people getting arrested, going to jail?"

That was Julian Bond, speaking over the phone and above the sounds of D.C. traffic while his wife piloted their car. Bond had a doctor's appointment that afternoon, and I offered to postpone our chat, but once he takes up the subject of the movement he doesn't like to stop.

We were talking about essences, constituent parts. I had classified three primary features of what Bayard Rustin, in a famous phrase, had called "the classical period" of the civil rights movement: the role of the church, the practice of nonviolent civil disobedience, and the widespread participation of young people. Others have arrived at this same configuration, one, it should be said, that is distinctly Southern, as activism assumed a slightly different shape in the North. Church was important there too, but other organs, such as labor unions, were available to concentrate awareness and activity. In Southern campaigns, a pattern emerged of the tactic of nonviolence being stressed by the church and then carried out by college and high school students. Occasionally, as in Birmingham, the participants were even younger than that.

"Yes," said Bond, "those are the elements that helped make it happen, but think about what it did: mobilization, litigation, organization, and coalition building. We do only some of those things now. We don't do coalition building as much as we ought to; litigation we still pursue, although with the conservatization of the Supreme Court and the federal courts generally, it's become a little more difficult to focus on that. Mobilization—if you look at the most recent [2012] election, there's tremendous turnout of black voters, and you can only hope that we'll do it in the next election and the next election and so on. And these are not new things. These are not brand-new things."

Now, I thought, we're getting to the heart of the matter, because one obvious question prompted by John Perdew's call for a movement was what would this movement look like—something old or something new? David Dennis had told me organizing was easier fifty years ago, before integration. In many Southern towns, the black community had functioned like an island; everyone lived in close proximity to one another and frequented the same shops and churches with a punctual regularity. Nowadays, Dennis said, a good deal of effort is spent trying to bring everyone together. So the issue at hand, I said to Bond, was not how do you get a movement started, it was how do you get a movement started in a world that has already been changed by the movement. The techniques we were discussing: would they serve us in our day as readily as they had that of Bond's youth?

That was when he mentioned the events in Raleigh, citing them as "a good example of the utility of nonviolence and how it's not out of fashion but very much in fashion. I'm just surprised," he went on, "that more people don't use it. It's easy to do, requires only a minimum of training, but for some reason people don't use it as much as I think they ought to or could."

The demonstrations Bond was referring to had begun in Raleigh, North Carolina, on Monday, April 29, 2013. That afternoon seventeen protestors entered the state's General Assembly building. They were told to leave, and when they did not, each one was arrested. Every Monday thereafter a march had been staged again, with the number of arrests steadily increasing; altogether there would be nearly a thousand before the legislature recessed in August. The weekly tradition was christened "Moral Monday," and it featured a dynamic, articulate leader, the Reverend William Barber II, president of the state chapter of the NAACP and pastor of a church in Goldsboro, North Carolina.

Barber likes to speak in a witty and epigrammatic style, and I have heard him explain the demonstrations by citing Sir Isaac Newton, saying that for every action there is an equal and opposite reaction. In truth the roots of Moral Monday are almost a decade old and the current demonstrations are a result of steady, ongoing organizing; but in making the Isaac Newton joke Barber was referring to state Republicans, who in January 2013 assumed control of both the governorship and legislature of North Carolina for the first time since 1870. Straightaway they voted to end federal unemployment benefits and the Earned Income Tax credit; eliminate tenure for teachers; deny the expansion of Medicaid offered by the Affordable Care Act; and repeal the Racial Justice Act, a law that allows minorities to challenge a death sentence if it can be proved that racism was a factor in the prosecution's pursuit of such a sentence. North Carolina immediately became known as a place to watch and was referred to again and again as a laboratory of Tea Party policy, which fulfilled one objective of the Moral Monday movement: to call attention to the agenda of the Republican bloc.

———

After Bond's endorsement, I felt I had no choice but to travel to Raleigh, and in July 2013 I witnessed the thirteenth Moral Monday. Before the march, a mass meeting was held in a nearby church, and as we filed in, I noticed the media sign-up sheet included reporters from the *Huffington Post*, the *Daily Beast*, and *Slate*. While the demonstrations had already begun to garner attention, the presence of the national media was also due to the timing of the march: it would take place one week after George Zimmerman had been found not guilty of the murder of Trayvon Martin and a month after the Supreme Court had struck down the coverage formula clause of the Voting Rights Act. That formula, which dates to the 1960s, names several states and counties that because of a history of voter suppression must seek approval or "preclearance" from the Justice Department before implementing measures that impact voting. Thirty-nine of North Carolina's counties were included in the formula, and now, released from the obligation of preclearance, Republicans had already drafted a voter identification bill, one that would drastically overhaul registration requirements as well as shorten the amount of time in which people could cast their ballot. Most agreed that the law's effect would be to keep a large number of African American and Hispanic voters away from the polls.

I had read that Bob Zellner was among those arrested on the first Moral Monday, and I decided to see if I could speak to him. Zellner had been SNCC's first white staff member, and a peculiar one to hold that distinction, since he had been raised by Klansmen, his father and grandfather both belonging to a klavern in south Alabama. Soon after being hired by SNCC, in October 1961, Zellner was swept up in activity surrounding an incipient voter registration project in McComb, Mississippi. One afternoon he was set on by a mob outside the courthouse in McComb and driven to a nearby jail; he spent the ride eyeing the noose that had been prepared for him. "They're coming to kill you," said the lawyer who drove down from Jackson to bail him out.

Zellner has a boyish quality, despite his age; he is restive and loquacious and sports a waxy, cherubic smile, one that can make him seem even now, as he embarks on his eighth decade, elfin. He draws a pension from the jobs he held after leaving SNCC but also relies on the generosity of friends as well as his own ingenuity or thrift. Some days he cooks over an open fire to spare himself the expense of lighting his stove. And the past is continually asserting itself in his speech. When I picked him up on the day of the thirteenth Moral Monday, for instance, he gestured behind him and said that two of the houses we saw were in the process of being converted to freedom houses. I had never encountered that term outside of a book. It conjured visions of all-night debates in smoke-filled cafés, youth and camaraderie, SNCC in its earliest, most innocent state.

Over lunch the habit continued, as we talked of the Trayvon Martin trial and the Supreme Court's ruling on section 4(b) of the Voting Rights Act. Zellner consolidates time in his answers, sees the present in the context of its many antecedents. "After the Civil War," he told me, "Reconstruction occurred, and between 1865 and 1885, nobody thought that we could go back to an all-white ballot box, and where people would be re-enslaved. They said you can't do that; it was impossible—and it took less than a generation to do it. By the beginning of the 1900s there was all white power. Well what's happening now? They're going against the vote again; everything that we won in the civil rights movement they are challenging, and right now, they're winning. And we thought, never again would it even be challenged. Fifty years later, in North Carolina, in Mississippi, all across the country, we're still having to fight the battles that we thought we had won in the First Reconstruction, and we thought we had definitely won in the Second Reconstruction. And it's now under attack again. That's why the Trayvon Martin case is so important. It told people: we're right back in Money, Mississippi, when a little boy is killed by adults and they go free."

I asked him to describe the first Moral Monday, and he said, "They couldn't resist—they simply could not resist the bait. That's what happens in the civil rights movement: You go as far as you can go. And then they say no. And then you say we're going to go anyway; we're going to find out what your limits are. We petitioned the governor through letters, personal visits, to meet and talk. They won't do it without preconditions, which are, okay, we'll talk as long as you don't criticize us and say bad things about us in public. And that's absurd. Of course we're going to say bad things about you, because you're doing bad things. So you continue to push the envelope. The first seventeen, all we had to do was go into the rotunda. It was a representative group of leaders, including a woman in a wheelchair. I happened to be holding her wheelchair at the time I was arrested, and even so, I was charged with holding a placard. And then they said afterwards, you cannot return to the legislature or you will be arrested simply for returning, for being there. So they played their role perfectly."

Here Zellner was articulating a major precept of movement theory, which is that your enemy is often your friend. Birmingham is not Birmingham—is not an incident that gets the country's attention—without the decision to turn on the hoses and send out the dogs. Selma, same thing, with the tear gas and the billy clubs wrapped in barbed wire. The more intransigent your opposition, as strange as it sounds, the easier it is to defeat, and the quickest way to disarm a movement is through compromise. We talked now of the Montgomery Bus Boycott and how modest the initial request had been. At first, leaders of the Montgomery Improvement Association sought only to eliminate the reserved space of the buses, the seats between the White and Colored sections that became, during rush hour, white only. Had the city fathers capitulated to this little demand, history would be very different.

"That's the difference," Zellner said, "between Birmingham and Mobile. In Mobile they were sophisticated enough to sit and talk. Mobile is not known as a movement town. Birmingham had Bull Connor. And the more rigid they became—you know, if you have a rigid structure and you hit a blow against it, it breaks. If you have a flexible one, like Mobile, it doesn't break. It simply gives.

But these people, this ultra-right wing in North Carolina, they were not interested in making any symbolic compromise, because they'd been pressed so far by the Tea Party."

And that was the perception nationally, I told him, that Moral Monday was born in response to the Tea Party. The remark frustrated him, and what he said next was reminiscent of what Maisha Moses had described, the fact that the work went on all the while, with no one ever knowing when or if the dam would break. "We wanted it," he said. "We planned for it. We made every effort to make it happen; we had no idea that it would. See, that's the difference, and it's very subtle, and you need to understand that. Your question makes me wonder if you understand. People have no historical context for anything anymore, and they think the whole thing is a spontaneous reaction to right-wing idiots in the legislature. It wouldn't be happening the way it is now if it hadn't been for six or eight years of grassroots organizing. There was a plan way back. Reverend Barber had organized at the grassroots—poverty tours: taking media, government groups, opinion makers, and so forth on a tour all over North Carolina, practically every county. That's when I got involved. I said, 'This man is serious.'

"When I retired I said, what could I do; I was thinking of going to New Orleans and relaxing. But North Carolina, that's where organizing is occurring—it has the roots, the shoes, the feet, in order to impress the entire nation; it's time for them to give to the nation the new image of organizing. We're organizing in eighteen districts now, and with sixty full-time organizers and financing, we're going to be able to do it over four election cycles. And we will change the South. We will change the nation."

Zellner's confidence was contagious. It was important to give America the new image of organizing, he had said, and now I couldn't wait to see it. Yet as we finished lunch and repaired to the church for the mass meeting that would go on before that Monday's protest, my assessment was that this new image looked a lot like the old. The fixtures were the same; the rhetoric was the same. Here we were in a Baptist sanctuary, singing freedom songs— "Ain't Gonna Let Nobody Turn Me Around"—and listening to a strategy session on nonviolence, what to do and not to do when the police handcuffed you, followed by a speech reassuring everyone of why their arrest was necessary in the push for voting rights. It was like slipping back five decades; the same work still needed to be done, and the same tactics would be deployed. Zellner stepped to the podium, put his arm around the guitarist, and led everyone in a chorus. This one went "Ain't going to let McCrory turn me around" in reference to Pat McCrory, the governor of North Carolina. "Turn me around, turn me around, turn me around," came the assembled reply.

Once the singing stopped, the media were asked to leave and the movement's legal team began addressing those who had volunteered to be arrested. The procedure was simple: at a certain point in the rally a path would be cleared from the stage to the statehouse, and the group was to march, single file, to the doors of the capitol, where the police would be waiting. The same plan had been carried out, more or less, each week for the past three months, and the police were as knowledgeable of the protocol as the protestors. Nothing could be easier, I thought, but when the lawyers asked if anyone in the audience had questions, there were so many that the exchange had to be cut short lest Reverend Barber lose the time allotted for his speech.

"I'm from out of town," said one. "Would I have to come back and hire a lawyer? I can't hire a lawyer."

This led to murmurs about legal fees. A woman sitting a few rows behind asked if her defense could cost as much as fifteen thousand dollars.

"And do we have to state our employer?" asked a man who feared his job would be threatened by publication of his arrest.

And on it continued, until someone in the church—and

remember, this was the most convivial of atmospheres—was moved to ask, "Well why are you here then?" Shouts followed, exclamations of "come on," and finally the questions ceased.

It should be remembered that this clash between resolve and circumspection—between a determination to do the right thing and a logical concern for the consequences that might arise—exists not only within an individual but within the movement entire, as I was to witness later that night. In the week leading up to this event in Raleigh, it seemed like all of America was marching. There had been demonstrations in several cities to protest the Zimmerman verdict. In Tallahassee, Florida, a group calling themselves the Dream Defenders, in a nod to King's speech at the March on Washington, had occupied the governor's office, demanding that a special session of the state legislature be convened to review Stand Your Ground, the law that earned national attention after being invoked in the instructions given to the jury during the Zimmerman trial. That night, after the Moral Monday march and rally had concluded and everyone was bailed out of jail, we returned to the church where the mass meeting had been held, and Reverend Barber went off to Skype with the Dream Defenders. Dinner had finished, and we were milling around the common room. I struck up a conversation with Curtis Gatewood, another Baptist preacher and North Carolina NAACP member who was instrumental in planning Moral Monday. While we were talking we were approached by a youth named Tyler who, inspired no doubt by the Dream Defenders, wanted to go and occupy the capitol in Raleigh—now, tonight.

"We're going down there," he announced. "Twelve of us."

"To do what?" Gatewood asked.

"Sleep. We'll be waiting when they get in in the morning. We'll call it the North Carolina Dream, or North Carolina Nonviolent Dream—what do you think of that; what if we add that we're nonviolent?"

Tyler's revolutionary zeal could not be guessed at by his appearance. He was dressed in a polo shirt, canvas cap and running shoes, not the garb you would expect of a young Turk, and the color of these articles was coordinated perfectly, the shade of blue and green in each identical. I never learned his full name. He could not have been older than twenty and had been present at every Moral Monday.

"You want to do it now?" Gatewood said.

"Now."

"So let's think that through. That kind of demonstration—"

"Is building off Moral Monday."

"Right—but what are you trying to accomplish? Give me the goal."

"Make a sign."

"Of what?"

"Resistance, unity. We're doing it for Trayvon."

"But is that the best way to go about it? Let's just run this through before you go down. What are other ways you might do that, and which is going to be the best?"

Tyler was silent. All the immediacy of his plan had been checked, and Gatewood assumed full elder statesman mode, coaxing yet firm: "See, that's what you got to ask yourself ahead of time: what do I want to accomplish, and what's the best way to go about it? I'm not saying it's a bad idea. We'll not rule anything out. All options are up. But maybe not tonight; maybe you don't go tonight."

A few minutes later Reverend Barber returned from the Skype call. And I thought I had witnessed something momentous, even though the conversation did not last long and scores like it were probably transpiring all around the church at the same time. I recalled what I had learned about the march from Selma to Montgomery. When that occurred, in 1965, the idea for it was a year and a half old. Diane Nash, one of James Lawson's Nashville students, had been so distraught by the Birmingham church bombing in September 1963 that she proposed to occupy the Alabama state capitol. Martin Luther King thought the plan too risky at the time, and it was tabled. King comes off in this example as a cautious pragmatist, yet it should be remembered that earlier in 1963, when the Birmingham campaign stalled, he enlisted thousands of that city's high school, middle school, and even elementary school students, urging them to protest and be arrested in defiance of segregation laws.

Seniority, in other words, may blunt the readiness of youth, focused as it usually is on the long run, but it will also turn to it for refreshment and a departure from its own relative timidity. John Perdew had told me that after he got married he had stopped marching and instead began working in SNCC's Atlanta office. "I was focused on building a marriage," he said, "and we soon had a child, so it would have been irresponsible of me to continue that front-line, foot-soldier kind of activity." Loyalties shift sooner or later—but youth, while it lasts, is free of those encumbrances involving job and family.

Both Tyler and Gatewood, I felt, were "right." The two perspectives—the impatience of one and the need for planning and forethought of the other—might seem at odds, yet the contrast between them, history has shown, can serve to hold the movement in balance. So in that little exchange I had seen something timeless; like the freedom songs heard earlier in the day, here was something else brought back from the past in its perennial and undiluted form. I felt like I had gotten a glimpse into the heart of things, as if a panel had been lifted and I could see the gears and knobs, all the workings that made the machine go.

———

Eating breakfast in a café the next morning, I read about Moral

Monday in the papers. And here it was again, the problem of doubleness; it sidled up to me at the countertop. Governor McCrory, I read, had dismissed Moral Monday for being comprised of outside agitators. "What, are you serious?" I exclaimed audibly from my seat. Fifty years, you'd think, would have been enough time to come up with a new term of dismissal. That was the very claim that excited denunciation from Southern governors way back when, and had been the reason John Perdew was sent to jail. All that remained was for the Republican leadership to say the motivation for the protests was for everyone to get their name in the papers. Well, I read on and discovered they had said that too.

Still, there were notable differences between the movement in Raleigh and the demonstrations it seemed to be so consciously modeled on. I may not have seen them right away, lost as I was in the spectacle of time travel—but they were there. Zellner was not the only example of sixties personnel floating around the scene, and I was also able to interview Margaret Herring, who joined SNCC in 1964. As a young and alluring white woman—she had been named a beauty queen in her hometown of Winston-Salem, North Carolina—the higher-ups at SNCC had judged her perfect for the task of espionage. Early in 1965 Herring was sent to Selma, where she pretended to be a reporter from *Parade* magazine. She was thus given an audience with the mayor and police chief and treated to a wealth of insider information. She lives not far from Raleigh now, and I asked her what the most striking difference was between that time and today. And she didn't hesitate, not even for a second. The fear, she said. The fear is no longer there. No one involved in Moral Monday had to worry about nightriders or attacks being perpetrated by policemen. Actually, Raleigh's police, many of whose officers were black, got on well with the protestors. Zellner seconded that when I asked him what it was like to be in jail again after so many years, following the first Moral Monday arrest.

"Well, I kept comparing it to my other nights in jail, and it was much better. They treated us courteously; some of them would wink at us. We were all together, men, women, black, white. They used to separate us four ways. All night we sang and prayed. Reverend Barber was very good; he would say, 'Okay, the women sing a verse,' and the women would sing a verse; he would say, 'Now the men sing a verse,' the men would sing a verse; he'd say, 'Now the police sing a verse.' There were twelve or fifteen policemen, and they all smiled. They almost sang! One policeman was heard to say, 'Oh my God we're all going to hell because we arrested the preacher for singing and praying!'"

On the Monday I met him, while we were driving to the church for the mass meeting, Zellner had assured me Reverend Barber was the next Dr. King, which seemed like a wild and un-realistic claim, one that had the effect of lowering my expectations. More of Zellner's retrospection, I told myself, since to find the next Dr. King is a chimerical errand; you'd do just as well to go out and search for a city of gold. To the church that Monday afternoon Barber wore a dark suit and glittering cuff links and walked with the aid of a cane, slumping, so that he gazed out from the tops of his eyes. His head, I noticed, wouldn't turn by itself. Any look to the right or left obliged him to shift his feet and move his torso in that direction, and these signs of frailty did not prepare me for what I encountered when he stepped to the podium.

"Forward together," he said, raising an arm, and the church resounded: "Not one step back!"

"Forward together!"

"Not one step back!"

The speech he gave was elemental, the classic preacher's speech, utilizing all the tools, the use of refrain, the catalogs of names and dates, suspense tightening in the sudden turn toward the climax, at which point the pace accelerates into the outburst, with the ensuing pause extended until it becomes weighty and the cycle can start anew. He had his work cut out for him: after voicing their qualms about bail bond and legal fees, everyone needed to be roused, ushered from the world of dreary practicality into some higher realm, and Barber did that. "This is a movement," he proclaimed, "not a moment," and the sermon built and built in intensity, one crest leading to another and still another.

"Truth of the matter is," he said about a recent election, "21 million votes, 18 million were tested, only found one case of fraud. Truth of the matter is, there's no problem with voter fraud. That's a lie; that's a distortion. If you're going to be regressive, at least be bold about it—don't act as though we don't know any better; don't act as though we don't know what's going on. We know what racism looks like; we know what injustice looks like"—the applause was building now, the crowd urging the riff onward— "we know what voter suppression looks like. We know what it looks like; we know what it walks like; we know what it talks like. These are extremists that want to go somewhere none of us want to go—and that's backwards."

He had to wait for everyone to settle down, and resumed: "The issue with this general assembly is not voter fraud; it's voter fear. They are afraid of all the voters voting."

From the pews came calls of "Watch it"; "Let him have it"; "Go ahead"; "Talk about it now"; "Tell the truth."

"They trying to pass a voter ID that's worse than Alabama, Georgia, Indiana, and South Carolina. In Alabama, if you a student, got an ID you can use it. Not in North Carolina. If you in South Carolina and you have a religious objection to being photographed, a disability or an illness, work schedule, lack of transportation, lack of birth certificate, family responsibilities, or any other obstacle you find reasonable, you can still vote. But not in North Carolina. Because they know if all the people vote, they won't be *in* the General Assembly, they'll be *out* of the General Assembly. We never needed voter ID for 237 years—why, all of a sudden, when black people are 25 percent of the electorate and Latinos are 24 percent, and we have the potential to have an electorate where black and brown people can come together like never before and transform the South, why all of a sudden are people cheating? Think about it now—they're saying, 'This can't be true; something wrong with electing a black president, something wrong with all these people coming together. They must be cheating.' Ain't nobody cheating. God has just fixed it for us to live long enough that hands that once picked cotton can now join hands with white hands and join hands with Latino hands and join hands with labor and join hands with gay and join hands with people all over the state and we can burst the solid South wide open, and we change the South, we change the Nation—and that's why we'll never go back!"

These last few words were barely audible, lost as they were in all the applause and shouting. Inspiration, I had cause to reflect, is largely a matter of the adrenal glands. For as Barber spoke I could feel the quickening inside of myself, and though I had come to the church to observe and evaluate, I was caught up in what movement people used to describe as a freedom high, buoyed, as if by hydraulics, on a grossly enlarged sense of my own indestructibility.

As we drove to the rally after Barber's speech, I said, "You know, there was a moment back there when everyone in the church was willing to do whatever he said." Zellner was in the car, as was a man named Kassa who worked for the NAACP. They both laughed and nodded. "No questions asked. He could have given the command, told us to rush the street, the town, whatever, and it would have been on."

———

The site of Moral Monday was the lawn connecting Raleigh's Wilmington and Salisbury Streets, and that placed the rally directly under the eye of the General Assembly, for the grass ran perpendicular to the statehouse. Its second-floor porch, I noticed, was thronged with spectators, with legislators and their staff looking down on the parade of speakers below. A thousand people or more filled the space between the stage and the Assembly. Many carried placards—I CAN'T BELIEVE I STILL HAVE TO PROTEST THIS SHIT!—although the farther one got from the stage, the more leisurely it was. People had brought their dogs, kids were hoisted onto the shoulders of their parents, and women drifted by in running shorts, giving the impression that Moral Monday was just something you did on a summer's day. Barber liked to call his campaign the Third Reconstruction, but I had also heard him refer to it as a fusion movement, and that term seemed the most apt, for everyone was given a berth at the rally, the roll-call of speakers coming alternately from the ranks of the poor, LGBT, and immigrant communities, advocates of reproductive rights as well as those who stood to be disenfranchised by the pending voter identification bill, Hispanics and African Americans. The crowd reflected a similar mixture. It was polyglot through and through, this movement, which finally amounted to the most significant difference between Moral Monday and its precedents from fifty years ago. Most of those who had volunteered for arrest were white, and there was nothing problematic or remarkable in this, no trace of the anxiety over white involvement that had engulfed the movement in the late 1960s. Moral Monday had been shorn of all that. It was a twenty-first-century phenomenon.

Several speakers preceded Reverend Barber, who was looser and more eager to tell a joke than he had been at the mass meeting, though his speech was just as inspired. When he finished, the cue was given, and the line of volunteers moved from behind the stage, through the crowd, and into the maw of police waiting by the door to the statehouse.

After their arrest, the rally moved to a small park on the other side of the government complex. Across the street were the school buses that those who had been arrested would board to be driven to the nearest jail. Cars drove around and honked, and people in Trayvon Martin T-shirts drifted by, making plans to rendezvous in another month at the fiftieth anniversary of the March on Washington. A roar went up when the first school bus pulled out. The others were not too far behind, and after the last had gone, I remained on the sidewalk with Zellner and a few dozen others. Reverend Barber had been invited to appear on MSNBC, but the show's taping kept being delayed. The freedom songs came back—"Eyes on the Prize," "This Little Light of Mine"—and we waited past the point when the heat broke and darkness thickened, and the cicadas wound up in the trees around us. At last the network gave the signal, and Barber sat in a chair while makeup was applied; as one production assistant leaned over with a brush and another slipped a pair of headphones over his ears, he lectured the anchor on how to interview him. "Don't say voter ID," he said. "It's voting rights." Once the interview started, I sat down beneath a tree with a canopy of leaves so full it blocked nearly all of the Raleigh skyline, and began making notes. I knew the interview had finished without looking up, for the songs had started again.

Julian Bond was right. Moral Monday had made nonviolence fashionable, and that was no small feat. In many discussions I'd been having, nonviolence was often the first thing dismissed. Nobody seemed to like it. The young romanticize confrontation and are frustrated by more orderly tactics they see as having no effect. Movement veterans, on the other hand, still seem to be haunted by the stereotype of the meek African American, and will go out of their way in an interview or reunion speech to discuss the guns that were present in the black community in the sixties, how they knew people who fired back one night, and so on. For a figure of Barber's stature to breathe new life into the tactic—an incommensurately powerful one, which had needed only a few weeks to dismantle Jim Crow in cities like Nashville and Birmingham—represented an exciting development and showed him to be a true student of history.

But the arrests in Raleigh had the feel of a pageant. The nonviolence that was loosed on Nashville and Birmingham had set those cities on edge, thrusting them into a mood of panic. One reason King loved the phrase "creative tension" was that he thought upheaval had to precede any lasting change. Yet here, in Raleigh, you had a script, executed with maximum ease and even something like courtesy. There were the police waiting at the door, the immediate posting of bond and processing of each arrestee, all of whom spent no more than five minutes in a cell and had returned to the church before I did. In the coming days, as I thought about what I had seen in Raleigh, the question that kept coming back for me was: just what was being put on the line here?

Zellner, during our talks, had said something interesting: the next step was to fill the jails. "Fill the jails" was Gandhi's tactic, and dates to the Salt March of 1930.* In this case it would mean more arrests, ten times as many at least—ten thousand a week—and a widespread refusal of bond. The strategy's premise is simple: overextend a town and drive it to a bargaining position. During the assault on Birmingham, for instance, the city ran out of jail space and money—but on it went, day after day; each morning there were more people to be ushered into the back of a paddy wagon. Stopping this constant procession, rather than preserving segregation, became the town's top's priority, and there was only one way to do that: take down the COLORED signs. But to fill the jails is risky; it's like burning your ships. The public is apt to turn

---

* In 1930, Gandhi led a long march in Gujarat, India, in protest of a British tariff. He went to jail for defying laws related to salt manufacture and possession, and tens of thousands followed him. "Fill the jails" subsequently became an important cry in the drive for Indian independence.

against you for creating such a spectacle and inconvenience, and if the lawmakers hold the line, the movement's resources—people and popular opinion—get consumed in the blaze. It's an all-or-nothing proposition, and in Raleigh there was a lot to be risked, at least in the short run. Since the start of the Moral Monday campaign, approval ratings for the Republican leadership had plummeted to a percentage in the 30s, and they had been in office for just half a year. Any change in tactic, then, could not be considered lightly, which Reverend Barber acknowledged when I shared with him what Zellner had told me.

"There are a lot of strategies to look at," he said. "What we did first, engaging in civil disobedience, we had no idea they would arrest us. The reality is, we didn't plan to do thirteen Moral Mondays. You always hope on the front end that if you go in and truly challenge people, and say: 'Look, I'm not challenging you because you're a Republican or a Democrat, I'm just talking about what's right and wrong,' then people will have a shift in consciousness. But then you find out in our state, they're so locked up in some ideological-historical time warp, trying to go back to a history that's gone, they arrest you. Well, first thing, before we talk about filling the jails up, you got to think about what we've had. You can't just run past that and say let's do something else. Nine hundred and forty-five arrests. We've had eighty thousand people show up. We've been able to organize in Mitchell County. It's 99 percent white, 89 percent Republican. And they are up there organizing, not just the NAACP but the people, to remove the Tea Party extremists, because they say they don't represent their kind of Republicanism. So we are in the process right now of evaluating the success of the movement and where we're going. But I know the movement won't stop; even if Democrats were to get elected tomorrow we got work to do with them."

A delicate answer, the sort of answer that is delivered on the record. You could say he was guarded, speaking to me as a member of the media and therefore choosing his words carefully, but it was clear at any rate that he knew how precarious the momentum of Moral Monday was, how much could be lost if its leader spoke out of turn.

Barber had arrived at our interview in his clerical attire, the black clothes and ring collar, as well as a cross made of twigs, a gift recently presented to him by fasting immigrants. In the time since that July Moral Monday I had learned that as a young man he was told he had ankylosing spondylitis, or arthritis of the spine, which explains his posture and gait, and because of that he will get up from time to time and tower over you, giving the interview the feel of a performance or a sermon. He will seize on a quote and vary it endlessly, displaying a gift, honed no doubt at the pulpit, for rhetorical handiwork. There is a slight hitch before this happens, a short pause or gathering; the eyes dilate slightly, and the swell begins. One must interrupt from time to time, as it seems the homily will last all day otherwise.

In conversation he cites books and historical reference continually, was even aware that the date of our meeting had been scheduled on what, in 1963, had been the third day of the children's crusade in Birmingham. Barber was born that same year, two days after the March on Washington. His parents were native North Carolinians but lived at the time in Indianapolis. His father, Barber said, "got a call from E.B. Wilkins, who was the principal of Union School in Roanoke. Schools still hadn't desegregated. E.B. called my father and said, 'Listen, you're one of ours; we need some help, we got to challenge this segregation.' My father saw it as a call, a Macedonian call, and he told my mother. Their commitment was to come back and begin working with black and white teachers, who would go to Elizabeth City State University and meet secretly, getting ready. I was at the time in segregated kindergarten or first grade. My father was one of the first science teachers to integrate the high school."

Barber learned about the movement the old-fashioned way, through firsthand experience: "People ought to realize the movement was everywhere—the movement's like a stream. We often talk about Greensboro, Montgomery, but there was movement in Wilson, North Carolina, and in Washington County; it just didn't make it into the newspapers. My home was filled with folks, and it was nothing for me to get into the car some days and my father would take me riding and I'd end up at Golden Frinks's house in Edenton, North Carolina, who was one of the lieutenants of Dr. King."

King is omnipresent in Barber's reflections, called on the most when explaining strategy and philosophy. Without necessarily trying to, Barber challenged one of the central tenets of movement wisdom—the one that frowns on charismatic leadership, holds that to be an undesirable. While America as a whole genuflects before King and regards him as a modern founding father, many in the movement find that problematic. They grant he performed a central task but begrudge his memory for the way it hoards credit for triumphs won, and the idea of a savior is generally held in low regard, for, as the saying puts it, "Strong people don't need strong leaders." One of SNCC's favorite metaphors was the reverse pyramid, indicating that power could run from the bottom up as opposed to the top down. But what became apparent while listening to Barber was that while all of that is true, the trouble comes when a duality is constructed, since both models can coexist and be effective. Barber himself rescued the charismatic leadership mantle: to the question of why this movement in this state and not any other, his presence would account for a substantial part of the answer.

I asked if he was bothered by the attacks on Moral Monday, the jibes that had been directed at him by the governor and other prominent state Republicans, one of whom had labeled the demonstrations "Moron Monday." Was thick skin something you develop over time? He said: "Being born in the family I was born in had an impact, watching the thick skin of my father, my mother, their commitment to justice, their commitment to all people, not just black people. But I think you're reborn; I think life calls you. Like right now in North Carolina, when you see a half million people—black, white, Republican, Democrat—being denied Medicaid expansion, 170,000 being denied unemployment, 900,000 being denied Earned Income Tax credit; when you see millions of dollars taken from public education, teachers being fired; when you see voting rights being attacked to the point that a woman like ninety-two-year-old Rosa Nell Eaton would not be eligible to vote under the current system; when you see people like that willing to fight, you develop a certain courage by being in the midst of courageous people. And the reality is, I don't really think we're so tough, when you consider the fact we come from people who stood up against slavery, who could get hung just for meeting. If they can stand up then, what keeps us from standing up now? In fact it would be a disowning and a disavowing of our birthright."

The guardedness was still there, I could see. Despite the passion and cogency of his language, he wasn't offering anything I couldn't hear at a rally or mass meeting. So I tried a new tack and read a quote by Bayard Rustin, planner of the March on Washington. "A demonstration," he remarked once, "should have an immediately achievable target. When a demonstration is just against being a black man in America, this is not a demonstration, it is a gimmick."

Barber did not like the implication of my choice to recite this. "Our movement," he said, "it's not agenda denied, it's actually deeply agenda rooted; we come together, we lay out our fourteen-point agenda of hope and not fear, addressing poverty, guaranteeing labor rights, education equality for all, health care for all, environmental justice, addressing the disparity in the criminal justice system as it relates to poor people and black people and other minorities, and expanding and protecting voting rights, women's rights, LGBT rights. So we have very specific objectives, and we have won on those objectives. After we march, we develop people's assemblies in local areas to keep up the pressure on legislators. When we went into the General Assembly and engaged in civil disobedience we were challenging this extremism, and the first goal of it was to shift the center of gravity of debate, a very specific goal. We had to establish a contract, capture the attention of the media so that people would wake up. Once people were awakened they came in masses.

"We also have a legal arm, so the things we rally about in the streets we find ways to get them in the court. It cannot be a moment; it cannot be just a march; it must be a movement with a moral narrative that puts a face and an agenda on the effort. Yes, every gathering ought to have an objective, but you can't always make the objective the next election or just this one bill. Our first objective was to shift the center of gravity. When we started they called us outsiders, they called us morons; the papers said it's just going to be another march. Now the papers are saying this is for real, people are not going anywhere, this is a sustained movement. Dr. King in 1961, before the AFL-CIO, said it's possible the only coalition that can fundamentally change America is when blacks and poor whites and labor and religious people and Latinos and others come together."

As absurd as I thought it had been for Zellner to call Barber the next King, I was willing to make the connection on this score. The most radical thing about King, I have always felt, was his inclusiveness; in 1967 and '68, when everyone in the movement was pushing inward, toward a greater homogeneity, he was going the other way, alienating half his staff for insisting that poor Appalachians, Native Americans, and Hispanics be brought into the fold. Scanning Moral Monday's diverse scene, it was easy to see Barber as continuing that mission, capable of inspiring the same sort of wide appeal.

"In a season like this," he said, "when there's so much pain—listen, you're in the South. Most of the poverty is in the South; most of the need for higher wages is in the South, but the people you are electing are fighting all the programs that would help uplift the poor, fighting the labor rights, fighting the health care. And you get white and black and other folks to start thinking about that not as Democrats or Republicans but as human beings, as moral agents, then you have the possibility of shifting."

———

Yet for all that, Barber is not fighting the same foe King was. John Perdew had said that in his day the enemy was blatant and therefore easier to combat. Today racial inequality is still institutionalized but concealed by euphemism, its existence much easier to deny. And so while Barber had revived the spirit of that time, could he fill the jails and win a retraction of the voter identification bill, or pressure the Republicans into accepting the Medicaid expansion? Can you burn your ships—can you risk everything, and put it all on the line—without a clear target on the order of a WHITE ONLY sign? It was the greatest question of any, and I wondered if the reason he hedged when I asked about it was not only because he was determined to be vague in front of a writer with his recorder on, but because he could not know the answer.

Sprung from the same city where SNCC had been founded, Moral Monday had focused the nation's attention on the Republican insurgency, and would surely have a hand in the 2014 midterm elections. That, in itself, was an impressive achievement. I wondered, though, if the movement was too mammoth and diffuse to hold. Its agenda was impossibly broad, containing the appeals of teachers, the unemployed, veterans, college students, and all those named in Barber's fourteen-point platform. Once, when asked what they were marching for in North Carolina, I paused a beat, wondering how I was ever going to structure my answer, until finally I replied: "Everything." There was no precise list of demands, no clear suggestion that I could find that had been advanced to the incumbent legislature. To the public—millions of unconverted—the petitions probably blended together in a clamor, I thought. And if you were for expanded unemployment benefits but against, say, abortion, what was your view of Moral Monday then?

Such a judgment, as we shall see, was not quite correct, yet even as I was wrong about Moral Monday I still knew it had a special power, one that went beyond the scope of ordinary political matters like party affiliation and midterm elections. In the summer of 2013, a reporter asked Barber what he hoped to accomplish with the Raleigh arrests. He gave a lengthy answer and spoke numinously, as King would, about "the hope of repentance" nonviolence offered, as a moment of cleansing for those who had made bad decisions. "The final thing," he said, "that civil disobedience does is it gives people a place to rally themselves, their energies, and their spirits, from deep within. People need these events, these Moral Mondays. They're going back to work like never before. It's almost evangelistic and revivalist. Transformative."

Barber's answer suggests a response to that quote by Rustin, which is that marching is its own end, a restorative act. Anyone who has ever participated in a mass demonstration, slipped into the humanity bath for an hour or two, can attest to this. At one march in Raleigh, called Historic Thousands on Jones Street—an annual rite that Barber started in 2007 and is now associated with the Moral Monday movement—at least sixty thousand people showed up. The procession stretched for blocks, and a couple hundred more were stuffed into the parking garages and office buildings lining the avenue. I stood shoulder to shoulder with men and women I might never meet or consort with in the ordinary course of life. Everyone was in agreement about where the country should be

headed, and confident—despite the reasons we had gathered—
that America would get there. One of the most powerful things the
movement can do, I reflected, was return one like this, if only temporarily, to a place of inspired faith, with the right path so clearly
laid out and the highest ideals seeming possible to attain.

The morning had been wintry and overcast, but at the end
of the march the sun emerged, an occurrence Barber couldn't
help but rejoice in. Everyone in the crowd linked arms and sang
a round of "We Shall Overcome," and Stevie Wonder's "Higher
Ground" was blasted through the speakers. Many began to move
in time, and as the song picked up and the sun washed over us,
Barber returned to the microphone. "Look at you!" he exclaimed.
"You're beautiful!" It was like a blessing, the preacher absolving
the multitude, all those who had been cast out and shunned, except
this horde was comprised not of hunchbacks and mendicants, as
it would have been in mythology, but of the plain folk of North
Carolina, its teachers and poor and women and immigrants. Later
my understanding of the significance of this scene, and of Moral
Monday as a whole, would change. But just now I was in thrall to
the power of the march, and I knew it was something mighty in
itself, regardless of what came of it. To influence approval ratings
or public opinion was well and good—but surely this, Barber's
benediction and the prevailing euphoria and patchwork of people
gathered, a group it might be impossible to summon on some other
occasion, was endgame enough. Yes, I thought, you can march
just for that.

3.

Howard Kirschenbaum is a retired academic. He taught education for many years at the University of Rochester, and was a psychology major at Johns Hopkins in Baltimore when he volunteered for the Mississippi Summer Project. He had participated in a few demonstrations organized by CORE, the Congress of Racial Equality, but like most Freedom Summer volunteers, his enthusiasm outstripped his experience, a disparity that Kirschenbaum, a member of a prosperous Long Island family, hoped the summer of 1964 would correct. He was assigned to Moss Point, a small town north of Pascagoula on the eastern side of the state, near the Gulf of Mexico. It was supposed to be one of Mississippi's safest towns— a relative distinction—and Kirschenbaum was disappointed to be going there, since he was looking for adventure, classical adventure in the heroic mold. He needn't have worried, for that is exactly what he got on his first night in the state, when he and another volunteer, Ron Ridenour, were picked up for vagrancy.

"We said, 'We've got thirty-five dollars in our pocket,' which was the threshold we were told to carry," Kirschenbaum recalled, "'and we have a place to stay.' They said, 'Vagrancy or we'll see what else.' They put us in the car, turned the lights out—by now it was close to dark—and accelerated to about ninety miles an hour down this Mississippi back road to a prearranged rendezvous point with another car. I can remember Ron saying to me, 'Do you think they're going to kill us?' Which was a logical question. We were the first people arrested after Schwerner, Goodman, and Chaney disappeared. But they had other plans for us, drove us at a more sensible speed to the jail in Pascagoula. On the way up to the third floor, where the cells were, as the elevator door closed the lights went out. I hunched my shoulders and tucked my head in, waiting for the blows to come. They didn't. When they brought us to the third floor we hoped they'd put us with black prisoners, which they did, but only for ten minutes. They moved us to the white prisoners' cell and pushed us in and said, 'Okay boys, here they are' and left the floor. The white prisoners had clearly been prompted to beat us, and somehow we talked our way out of it; we convinced them we weren't in Mississippi to get their sisters to marry blacks, and it was voting rights: 'Shouldn't everybody be able to vote in America, isn't that the right thing?' And they weren't going to do the police any favors anyway."

Kirschenbaum was released in the morning. He spent much of that summer, as he said, trying to register voters. He walked to the courthouse in Moss Point with any African Americans who were willing, and stood in line as they waited to meet with the registrar.

"We didn't succeed much," he told me. "One day about fifty folks marched to the courthouse to register; nobody was even let in to take the test. Did it again another day and a whole bunch of people were arrested. Ten of them were put in the back of a station wagon. The police had to push the door closed to squeeze everybody in, and they were left out in the hot Mississippi sun for two hours while one of the policemen stayed with a shotgun pointing at them, joking about how easily accidents happen. So this was the safe part of Mississippi. We tried to start a new registration drive in another part of town. Somebody allowed us to stay in their apartment. The next day they were evicted. People lost their jobs for supporting us."

Summer Project organizers knew that would occur; none of

the events Kirschenbaum detailed were unique to him or to Moss Point. The same story had been playing out endlessly in Mississippi since 1961, when SNCC began its first registration drive in the state. That was why the Council of Federated Organizations (COFO), the group in charge of the Summer Project, had established a political party of its own, the Mississippi Freedom Democratic Party. Signing up for that was easy, or at least easier. Volunteers like Kirschenbaum could take down names after explaining what the party was. Few of Mississippi's African Americans had ever participated in an election, and in many cases their knowledge of the political process was nil. The Mississippi Freedom Democratic Party was meant to be a simulation, a practice or trial run of democracy—until August 1964, when it became very real, as the party sent its own delegates to the Democratic National Convention in Atlantic City, New Jersey.

"The most meaningful experience I had in Mississippi," said Kirschenbaum, "the thing I remember the most, was the precinct meeting for the Freedom Democratic Party. There were three people in my precinct, one of whom was a big, tall, solid black sharecropper. He was wearing an immaculate pair of overalls and a white T-shirt. He was very uncomfortable in the world of parliamentary procedure; he didn't speak much during the meeting, probably didn't have much of an education beyond third or fourth grade. But when it came time for somebody to officially nominate the delegates who would go to Atlantic City, he volunteered. And he stood up and read the card. 'I nominate Lyndon Johnson for President of the United States.' There were tears in his eyes. For the first time in his life—I think I'm accurate in interpreting—he felt he was participating with full dignity, a citizen of the democracy of the United States."

In a short span, three months between his sophomore and junior years of college, Kirschenbaum witnessed the entire voting rights struggle in concentrated form, particularly the futility, the courthouse barring its doors, and the reprisals dealt those who supported the summer volunteers.

———

It is a delicate question, how remote that time is from our own. A year after the Mississippi Summer Project, the Voting Rights Act was passed and registration became a federally monitored activity. Blacks in the South could vote and run for office. But there used to be a saying in the movement: You can't legislate feeling. Legally, that is, people can be forced to act in a way they would not choose to on their own, and the question is whether, without the continuing oversight of legislation passed fifty years ago, lawmakers in the South would behave any differently today. A recent decision by the U.S. Supreme Court makes this much more than an academic question.

In 2010 Shelby County, which is located in the middle of Alabama, along the southern edge of Birmingham, filed suit against the Justice Department, with Attorney General Eric Holder named as defendant. Their action challenged the constitutionality of Section 5 of the Voting Rights Act, the preclearance provision, as well as Congress's right to reauthorize the Act, which it had done in 2006. Shelby County was covered by section 4(b) of the Voting Rights Act because of its history of keeping African Americans away from the polls. That meant it had to obtain "preclearance," a formal stamp of authorization from the Justice Department, before implementing changes to its voting laws or registration procedures.*

The U.S. District Court and Court of Appeals ruled against

———

* When applying for preclearance, the burden falls on the district or county to show any proposed change "neither has the purpose nor will have the effect" of blocking one's right to vote because of race.

the suit. But on June 25, 2013, the Supreme Court sided with Shelby County by a vote of 5 to 4—though not in the way many were predicting or feared. When ruling on *Shelby v. Holder*, the justices did not strike down section 5, but chose to eliminate the coverage formula. Preclearance still exists, but no one is required to submit to it any longer.

In authoring the opinion for the majority, Chief Justice Roberts portrayed the Voting Rights Act as an anomaly that could no longer be condoned. Federal intrusion into an area constitutionally apportioned to the states—the handling of elections—had once been warranted, but was no longer, he wrote. He characterized preclearance as a double breach of federalist philosophy. First, it accorded special treatment to some states, those in the Deep South that fell under the coverage formula, and second, it gave Washington the power to veto a state's law before it took effect, reversing the normal order of things. Both protocols, in his view, ran contrary to the spirit of the framers of the Constitution.

In those states that had been covered by the formula, the percentage of whites and blacks who are registered to vote is now about the same, and that, wrote Roberts, makes the coverage formula outdated; today, he said, it seems random and unfair, although the Chief Justice appeared to understand such logic locked him in a Catch-22. "There is no doubt that these improvements are in large part *because of* the Voting Rights Act," he said. "The Act has proved immensely successful at redressing racial discrimination and integrating the voting process." Yet those redresses were then given as the reason why preclearance was no longer defensible: "The formula captures States by reference to literacy test and low voter registration and turnout in the 1960s and early 1970s. But such tests have been banned nationwide for over 40 years. And voter registration and turnout numbers in the covered States have risen dramatically in the years since. Racial disparity in those numbers was compelling evidence justifying the preclearance remedy and the coverage formula. There is no longer such a disparity." By curtailing discriminatory habits to the degree that it did, in other words, the Voting Rights Act snuffed out its own need.

In her dissent, Ruth Bader Ginsburg noted this odd dimension to the case. "In the Court's view, the very success of Section 5 of the Voting Rights Act demands its dormancy," she wrote, and went on to name examples why she thought the coverage formula still necessary. The debate, in short, falls on which Justice has the accurate pulse of history. Roberts thinks the changes wrought in the last fifty years are permanent, that a discrepancy in those states originally marked for coverage will not return. Ginsburg believes that once the safeguard of preclearance is removed, Southern precedent will revert to form, and we'll witness something akin to the Wild West of old, when states were endlessly creative in finding ways of stripping blacks of the franchise. Along this line, she stressed that voter suppression did not end in 1965. The years following passage of the Voting Rights Act, Ginsberg wrote, saw the rise of second-generation barriers, or "efforts to reduce the impact of minority votes, in contrast to direct attempts to block access to the ballot." Gerrymandering* is the most common kind of second-generation barrier. Both parties engage in it, and in either case race is usually the key to the map, the reason why districts have been drawn up the way they are.

It is too early to describe with finality the effects of the *Shelby v. Holder* decision and the de facto elimination of preclearance. Yet it should be noted that the bill passed by the North Carolina legislature and signed into law only months after the *Shelby* decision

---

* The practice of drawing district lines in a way that favors one party. Districts are set every ten years, based on census data, and in deciding their boundaries the incumbent majority will usually try to create a spread of votes that will make it easier for the incumbents to stay in office.

would not seem to fall into the second-generation category. It does not attempt to minimize the power of votes cast by blacks and Hispanics and other citizens of color, but seeks to block exercise of the franchise in the first place, by imposing obstacles to registration. The Justice Department moved on the law right away, filing suit against North Carolina—and against Texas, which passed similar legislation after the announcement of the *Shelby* decision—in September 2013. The department challenged the articles that have traditionally discouraged minorities from voting: the insistence on photo identification and the elimination of early voting and same-day registration.

Governor McCrory said the new law would guarantee "no one's vote is disenfranchised by a fraudulent ballot," but most experts concluded the opposite. "The North Carolina measure is the most sweeping anti-voter law in at least decades," wrote Rick Hasen, the author of *The Voting Wars: From Florida 2000 to the Next Election Meltdown* and a professor of law and political science at the University of California at Irvine. "I'm not big on using the term 'voter suppression,' which I think is overused and often inaccurate, but it is hard to see this law as justified on anti-fraud, public confidence, or efficiency grounds. The intent here is to make it harder for people—especially non-white people and those likely to vote Democratic—to register or cast a vote that will be counted."

During my interview with Reverend Barber, I wondered aloud if the voter ID law wasn't part of a death throe. America is not getting any whiter, after all, and the Republicans' brand of political appeal, the Tea Party, will sooner or later have to broaden out to address the body politic of the twenty-first century. But in the meantime they can attempt to consolidate their base and carry on a few more years. Maybe, in addition to everything else, the North Carolina bill was an act of desperation or denial?

"Extremists in this state are operating out of fear," Barber replied. "They see things changing. They see an electorate evolving in the South, so what they're trying to do while they have the chance is do as much damage as they can. And it's always that case. When George Wallace stood in the schoolhouse door—he wasn't winning. He was losing. Franklin Delano Roosevelt, they called him a crippled communist and a socialist when he was pushing the New Deal. They weren't winning. The white Southern strategy, they developed it because they were losing, and it's worked for years, but all of that stuff eventually falls apart, as long as the movement continues."

John Lewis agreed. "They're sailing against the spirit of history," he said. "You cannot stop what has happened in America." A couple months after the Court announced its decision in *Shelby v. Holder*, I went to see Lewis, the most visible human symbol of the Voting Rights Act. It was Lewis who led the column of marchers across the Edmund Pettus Bridge in Selma, Alabama, on March 7, 1965. He later wrote that he did not expect to survive the attack that ensued, named "Bloody Sunday," during which an Alabama trooper billy-clubbed him in the skull; Lewis collapsed on the ground and cannot remember how he got back across the bridge, which was in a fog of tear gas. A week later, President Lyndon Johnson addressed both branches of Congress and introduced the Voting Rights Act. Alone among congressmen, Lewis can personally claim a piece of the legislation that brought him to where he is; he was elected to the House of Representatives in 1982, and the phrase "won his seat" takes on new meaning in his company. He is in Washington because he marched and almost died for the right to vote, and the office that he occupies across from the Capitol does not seem like a bad trophy.

That office is a monument to the movement, with black-and-white pictures covering one wall and all sorts of keepsakes—including a Wheaties box with Lewis's likeness on it—under glass. One photograph shows him lying on the ground with Martin Luther King, taken during the march from Selma to Montgomery.

A large, spidery bandage is fixed to Lewis's head, a sign of the March 7 attack. Those two met when Lewis was eighteen, for it was at one time his aspiration to integrate Troy State University, a college located a few miles from the farm in southern Alabama where Lewis's family worked as sharecroppers. He detailed his plans in a letter to the Southern Christian Leadership Conference,* and in the summer of 1958 was summoned to Montgomery for a meeting with King and Ralph Abernathy. But the plan never came off, as Lewis decided it was too risky for his family. "As the weeks passed that summer," he was to say, "my mother became more and more afraid that they would lose their land, or that their credit at the feed and seed store would be canceled. My father was driving the county school bus by then—the same bus I'd ridden to school each day as a boy—and my mother was afraid he might lose that job."

Lewis finished his education in Nashville instead, at American Baptist Theological Seminary, where he fell in with Bevel, Nash, Lafayette, and others whose ambition was being shaped by James Lawson and his weekly workshops. Next Lewis commenced a tenure unmatched by anyone in the movement. He is the only one to have participated in every major campaign of the 1960s. He led the Nashville sit-ins and was present at the founding of SNCC. The following summer, in 1961, CORE selected him to be one of the original Freedom Riders. He spoke at the March on Washington and helped oversee the Mississippi Summer Project, and after that came Selma. And then came SNCC's civil war: As the organization moved to expel white members, sponsor black nationalism, and reject its former acceptance of nonviolence, Lewis, who was leery of such developments, was voted out of his position as chair-

---

* An organization founded in 1957, following the victorious bus boycott in Montgomery, Alabama. As its name suggests, the Southern Christian Leadership Conference was comprised mainly of preachers who hailed from black churches in the Deep South; King led the group until his death in 1968.

man. He was only twenty-six, yet had already borne a lifetime of trial and witness.

To step onto the patio of Lewis's office in Washington, D.C., and behold the dome of the Capitol, its pillars and breadth and corrugated marble front, is a storybook experience, for you realize his life possesses the roundedness and instruction of a parable: the child of sharecroppers who put his life on the line for his people and became a national lawmaker. When you interview him, you are forced to give up all hope of a solitary face-to-face. His press secretary lords over your every move, and people are constantly coming in to pay their respects, to stand with the congressman and have their picture taken. A television displays the proceedings on the House floor, with a chime signaling when he must break away and record a vote. Fifty years after Selma, he can seem less like a person than a personage. It is impossible to escape the archetypal dimension of his being, the mythic quality noted above, and he has been consulted on voting rights so many times that inevitably he sounds, here and there, like a press release. The sound bites emerge readymade, and have no need of an editor. But he is not a careless or indifferent subject; he acts as though you are the only one in the room—all that commotion and hullabaloo aside—his gaze never straying from yours and his voice ponderously pitched, the speech delivered in a low, dulcet tone that recalls the barrens of Alabama.

I had interviewed Lewis before, but the meeting I am describing now took place on September 13, 2013, two days before the fiftieth anniversary of the Birmingham church bombing. "The morning the church was bombed," he told me, "I was in Alabama visiting my family, and I received a call from Atlanta. We heard about the bombing, and I took a Greyhound bus. My folks were so afraid they had an uncle of mine drive me sixty miles below Troy, to Dothan, then come back through Troy, so no one would recognize me. Still on the bus, go through Montgomery, then to Birmingham."

We discussed the realities of that time, when a church being dynamited was almost an everyday thing. Fear and violence had distinguished Lewis's youth, and he had been reminded of that during another recent commemoration, the fiftieth anniversary of the March on Washington. "August 28, 1963, came out of struggle," he said. "It's hard to compare. It's so different. People came fresh from jails. Many had been beaten and arrested in Birmingham, in Mississippi, in Tennessee, in Georgia."

It would be crude, in other words, to align that time with our own, and yet soon that was exactly what we were doing, once the topic turned to voting rights, Moral Monday, and the Dream Defenders. Said Lewis, "The techniques and tactics that we used during the late fities and the sixties—they're not obsolete. Dr. King used to say there's not anything more powerful than the marching feet of a determined people. When you engage in nonviolent protest, in North Carolina or at the state capitol in Florida, peaceful, orderly, it's a form of persuasion, a form of educating the larger community. I remember President Johnson saying to Dr. King back in 1964 or '65 we didn't have the votes in Congress to get a Voting Rights Act passed. He said to Dr. King, 'Create the climate, create the environment, make me do it.' And that's what we did."

Here it was again, the sense of doubleness, the vortex I had fallen into during my talk with John Perdew. Both perspectives were detectable in Lewis's speech, the differences between today and 1963 on the one hand and the similarities on the other. Time to go out again and advocate for voting rights, he was saying, using the same techniques as before. And I realized that in putting it to me the way he did, Lewis had communicated something profound about how change is wrought in a democracy like ours—who leads, who follows, and how spectacularly rare it is for change on the order of the Voting Rights Act to originate from within the Beltway. "Create the climate," LBJ had said. "Make me do it." And they had: Selma and the spectacle of Bloody Sunday accrued a power greater than that of the Oval Office and put Lyndon

Johnson temporarily at the mercy of the movement. He may have been president, but his hand was not on the tiller.

From that we can infer that in its best moments the movement creates its own reality. When it succeeds, it does so not because it has been adjusted to fit political reality, a world of pragmatism and compromise and tit for tat, but because it has bent that reality somewhat closer to its own. The lasting importance of Greensboro and Selma lies in the way those campaigns managed to close the distance, to merge existing conditions with a higher vision, and with such alacrity, too, gripping the country and ushering it along at a pace faster than its chosen speed. That is not accomplished by following the rules or appealing to customary methods. Taking a lobbyist to the Capital Grille and to courtside seats at a Washington Wizards game, gradually earning a measure of support for a bill but then watching it get waylaid by committee . . . it is natural to be wary of this process, and for a simple reason: it's like entering a casino. The odds are stacked. As Lewis's mentor, James Lawson, recently remarked, "Today, much of our activism does not discuss, study, and apply what nonviolence theory offers the struggle. Too much activism gears itself to lobbying legislatures and Congress and the president. That activism does not have the clout that the Council on Foreign Relations has, or that Exxon has or the Pentagon has, so it's lost. Again and again, when a movement begins to raise its head in the United States, the so-called political social progressive forces immediately try to surround it and guide it into the channels they think are important."

For Lawson the answer is simple, or it sounds simple: don't play the game. Don't bet the odds. Or at least don't expect meaningful change to come of it if you do.

And I wonder whether anyone ever had less of an expectation of ending up in that world, the world of lobbyists' dinners and party caucuses, than John Lewis. "I think the young people in the Student Nonviolent Coordinating Committee represented something very special," he said during our visit. "They were on the front line; they were the shock troops, the real soldiers of the movement." Lewis had once been leader of that battalion. He represented SNCC at the March on Washington, gave a speech that, even incorporating the handful of edits that were demanded at the last minute, startled with its fierceness. "We are now involved in a serious revolution," he said. "This nation is still a place of cheap political leaders who build their careers on immoral compromises and ally themselves with open forms of political, economic, and social exploitation." If King's "I Have a Dream" speech, delivered a few hours later, was notable for its promise of hope and reconciliation, Lewis took the opposite course, stating that the movement planned to reenact Sherman's march to the sea and "burn Jim Crow to the ground—nonviolently."

Now, as we sat in his office reflecting on that time, on the March on Washington and the Birmingham church bombing, we could hear a line of picketers making their way down Independence Avenue. A small rally for immigrant reform was being held. Up on the second floor, we could not see anything as yet, but the chants were audible through the patio window. The bells started chiming outside Lewis's office, and he broke away to record a vote. I left too. Outside, the road was closed, and around me were a hundred or so women, clothed in matching T-shirts and holding up signs. They paused before the Cannon Building, where several representatives, in addition to Lewis, keep an office, and began shouting, three separate cries gradually merging into one, the placards jabbing in time. This scene made me think about Lewis, the patterns of his life, and its unlikely, storybook reversals. Given his choice in the arrangement of things, I wondered, where would he rather be—out here, with the masses and marchers, or over there, in chambers, casting that ballot yea or nay?

———

It was not long after leaving Lewis that afternoon that I realized I had gotten Moral Monday wrong, misjudged the phenomenon of it. I had thought it ungainly, diffuse, but I had been looking at it the way a pundit or lobbyist might; that's what comes from hearing the clichés of our political discourse, the chatter about courting the vote and scripting agendas for the upcoming election cycle. Movement leaders, I realized, don't think like that, or at least they don't think like that all the time. The truth was that the movement in Raleigh aimed to rise above the political lay of the land—and that was a deeply historic act.

"America," Barber had told me, "has this strange tendency to step forward and hiccup, go backwards, come forward; America has always had this strange thing of compromising on our values. That's how we ended up three-fifths of a person. But nothing in this country has ever transformatively happened without a moral center. See, what has hurt us with the movement is Dr. King and others left us with a legacy of a moral movement. We've gotten caught up in left-right, Republican-Democrat, red-blue, conservative versus liberal; we've got caught up in using this language, and the problem with that is civil rights is not a left issue or a right issue; it's a moral issue. You know, treating women right is not left or right; it's moral. Treating children right is not left or right; it's moral. Our goal is not to be a thermometer, where we just say: What does the media want? What's popular in the polls? We must be thermostats; we must have an independent, indigenously led, deeply moral coalition."

It was the ultimate test to marshal such a coalition and keep it away from the extenuations of political maneuvering, those channels Lawson referred to. A lot would have to happen, to break just right, for Moral Monday to sustain its present form and momentum, but at least now the test could be run, and that was an important first step.

Meanwhile, I reflected, it should avoid settling for old illusions—even if contemporary events were pushing in that direction. Fifty years ago, the movement seemed to be proceeding in a stepwise and logical manner. First came the desegregation order for schools. That allowed for a broader push towards the integration of public accommodations. Once Jim Crow was out of lunch counters and department stores everyone was free to turn their attention to the ballot. Nineteen sixty-five and the Voting Rights Act looked like the brink. The humiliations of daily life had been routed, and it was time for the frontal assault. Political power was close at hand, and the vote would open up a new and more equitable America.

Yet the vote was not the gateway to that America. History tells us as much, though we did not need history, for at the time a few understood already this would be the case—and not just any few, but the principals involved in guaranteeing the ballot to begin with. In June 1965, while the Voting Rights Act was circulating through Congress, Lyndon Johnson addressed the graduating class at Howard University. "Freedom is not enough," he told them, and went on: "We seek not just freedom but opportunity—not just legal equity but human ability—not just equality as a right and a theory but equality as a fact and as a result." The date and audience assembled make this seem like more than your typical case of political grandstanding. "This is the next and more profound stage of the battle for civil rights," Johnson said.

And if that was the conclusion in the ivory tower of Washington, the same judgment was being fashioned in the hold of the struggle. Robert Moses, the director of the Mississippi Summer Project, grew up in a housing project in Harlem yet had never encountered privation on the scale of what he witnessed in Mississippi, particularly in the Delta, the agricultural plain stretching from Memphis to Vicksburg. He saw the poverty, the shotgun tenements and the schools, anemically funded and rundown. Black sharecroppers worked the Delta's plantations year-round, and their level of schooling rarely inched above the elementary grades.

"There was nothing really that prepared me for the level of education that we encountered in the Delta," Moses told me recently, and that made me ask whether, as he canvassed and marched to the courthouse and performed other tasks associated with registration, he was also—and perhaps unconsciously—formulating a strategy to tackle the problem of the schools.

"Actually, no," he said after a moment's reflection. "What I was thinking was we have to figure out a way to have our own resources and money."

"And that was the vote, right?"

"Well it didn't turn out be to the vote," came the reply. "After it was clear we were going to get the vote, I was thinking: we don't have a way to actually generate resources, funds, money, to control how we work, what we want to work on."

Like Jim Crow, the vote had given people something to rally around, and as the debate over access to the ballot returned in 2013 and 2014, I detected more than a trace of the old mythology, the elevation of the vote into some magic tool, or the final summit that had to be scaled before catching a glimpse of the promised land on the plain below. Yet, since we've all seen this movie before, there is little reason to expect a new ending. Mississippi, after all, is the state with the most black elected officials, and Moses and others can claim that as their legacy, but it is still the poorest state, with woeful outcomes in education and health care. As a young field secretary for the NAACP put it, "We have been able to pierce the political sphere but not the economic sphere." And that was the greater tragedy of the *Shelby* decision and the timeless, double-vision quality of our present moment: the vote is not enough, yet the movement had to keep returning to it, as if being driven back on itself.

PART TWO

Filling in the Gaps

I.

Here's a story, one that is about history's gaps, its lacunae and why they exist. It takes place during a kinetic time, the same years as the Montgomery Bus Boycott and the desegregation of Little Rock's Central High. But the events in the story are of the guerrilla or underground variety. They transpired without much notice, particularly at first. One is tempted to call it a counter-story, but to do that is to subordinate it, to designate it as secondary or alternate, and that is one of the subjects at hand: how some stories come to be regarded as main or central, while others are left behind and forgotten.

It begins in May 1954—or maybe 1956. You can draw the line at either point. After the Supreme Court handed down its decision in *Brown v. Board of Education*, states in the South began devising ways of eliminating the NAACP.* In 1956 Alabama's Attorney General, John Patterson, ordered the NAACP to hand over the names of its members. When the group refused, a circuit judge ruled that it could no longer conduct business in the state. That same year, South Carolina passed a law that made it illegal for any

---

* The strategy was fatally nearsighted, as it would turn out, for black activists simply adopted new configurations. The NAACP would lose thousands of members in the late 1950s, and several chapters would fold, yet the purging coincided with the birth of the organizations we associate with the civil rights movement of the following decade, the Southern Christian Leadership Conference and the Student Nonviolent Coordinating Committee.

employee of the state, or one of its cities or counties, to belong to the NAACP. The move targeted teachers, who were vital to local chapters, often serving as secretary or membership chair. For them the new law meant a choice between resigning their membership and losing their job.

In response, one of Charleston's teachers mailed a letter to seven hundred others, calling on them to join her in defying the statute, for if they all stood together, she reasoned, the state would be forced to let the law lapse into abeyance, unenforced. They could not, after all, afford to gut an entire profession. This teacher, whose name was Septima Clark, had scheduled an appointment with the superintendent, which would be the perfect time for all the teachers to gather and show their unity and force. But on the appointed day only five showed up. There would be no mass protest, and when she was compelled by the new law to list the organizations to which she belonged, Clark included the NAACP. The school board of Charleston voted not to renew her contract.

Clark was a native of Charleston, born in 1898. Poinsette, her maiden name, came courtesy of her father's master, Joel Roberts Poinsett, a statesman who had served in the House of Representatives and also been appointed Minister to Mexico. After he was manumitted as a result of the Civil War, Clark's father, Peter Poinsett, moved to Charleston and worked as a waiter and janitor. Clark's mother was Haitian and a bit of a taskmaster. They lived in a mixed neighborhood, alongside German, Italian, and Irish immigrants. Clark attended a private school, the Avery Normal Institute, and passed the state's examination for teachers as early as the tenth grade; it seems she never had designs on another profession. The principal of Avery urged her to go to college, but her family could not afford it, so after graduating in 1916, Clark took a job on Johns Island, a seahorse-shaped mass to the west of the Charleston peninsula, the largest in a chain of islands that forms the eastern edge of South Carolina's Low Country. She did not have much choice, as the city of Charleston forbade African Americans from teaching in its schools, even in those reserved for black children.

Johns Island is not ten miles from Charleston, and today you can drive there in a matter of minutes, but a bridge connecting it to the city was not built until after World War II. The sort of life that was carried on in such isolation shocked Clark. Most of the island's residents were black and worked on cotton and rice plantations, "virtual slaves," she recalled; a few owned their own farms but lived hand-to-mouth as well, unable to save money. There was no doctor on the island—the closest lived on the one adjoining, Wadmalaw—and people used folk remedies to treat ailments, such as applying spider webs to small abrasions. Privies were few, and the island's residents tended to relieve themselves in the bushes, a practice that contaminated the water supply, which came from surface wells. Pellagra, born of vitamin deficiency, was common, and mosquitoes prospered in the swampy climate, carrying infections and preying especially on babies, who were left alone for hours at a stretch while their mothers worked in the fields.

The Promise Land School, where Clark taught, had an official count of 132, whereas the white school in the same area held just three students.* Clark was principal and in charge of grades five through eight. Chalk and textbooks were in short supply, and Clark brought paper dry-cleaner's bags over from Charleston, using them to copy out stories the children told her in the island's own idiom, Gullah, a mixture of African, English, and European speech. The students would kneel on the floor, lay a page on the wooden bench above them, and write the tales out in their own hand, rising sometimes to fetch a log for the stove or clasp the shutters when the wind rocked through the little building. Every-

---

* As it happens, the color of the buildings served as a kind of indicator of who was being taught where. One was whitewashed and the other was creosoted, making for a black exterior.

thing bowed before the economic realities of the island. Several of Clark's students did not report to school until November or even later, since they were needed to help out with the harvest; and they would leave again in February or March, once planting season began. As they got older, many stopped attending school altogether, and often, any habits of reading and writing they acquired were lost.

Health care and education, then, were substandard, yet on Johns Island there flourished a dynamic local culture, particularly in the realm of music. Songs were created from the ancient instruments of voice and hand, with intricate polyrhythms. African American music of the Low Country was some of the first to impinge on white consciousness, and the island's songs were documented, to one degree of accuracy or another—Gullah's subtleties escape exact transcription, and so does the tradition's melodic style—in books such as *Slave Songs of the United States*, published in 1867, and *Army Life in a Black Regiment* by Thomas Wentworth Higginson. "Often in the starlit evening," Higginson wrote of his time as commander of the First South Carolina Volunteers, a black company in the Civil War, "I have returned from some lonely ride by the swift river, or on the plover-haunted barrens, and, entering the camp, have silently approached some glimmering fire, round which the dusky figures moved in the rhythmical barbaric dance the negroes call a 'shout,' chanting, often harshly, but always in the most perfect time, some monotonous refrain."

Clark, we can be sure, heard the shout during her time on Johns Island. When she started at Promise Land, a praise house had just been finished, Moving Star Hall, which was the site of many religious observances, such as the "watch night meetings" that occurred on Christmas Eve and New Year's Eve, when singing and dancing would last from midnight till sunup. Clark left Johns Island in 1918 and moved back to Charleston when she was offered a job at Avery. Before that, however, two things happened that would permanently alter her life. One was that she began teaching adults how to read, in the evenings after supper, when there was nothing left to do in the fields. Two, she attended a meeting where a group of preachers spoke about a young organization, the NAACP, that was recruiting members. Looking back years later, Clark would write, "It was the Johns Island folk who, if they did not set me on my course, surely did confirm me in a course I had dreamed of taking even as a child, that of teaching and particularly teaching the poor and underprivileged of my own underprivileged race." Clark would repay the debt; she would return to Johns Island several years later, and it would be the place where she would make her greatest impact, as both an educator and a figure of prime importance in the civil rights movement.

Back in Charleston she witnessed the power of the NAACP immediately. The organization had begun lobbying the city to repeal its ban on black teachers. In response the school board claimed that only mulattoes—that is, patrician blacks—wanted their children to attend schools staffed by African Americans. Clark helped gather signatures from parents averring the opposite. These petition cards proved decisive in a hearing held in January 1919, when South Carolina's House of Representatives ordered the school board to begin hiring black teachers. A sense of congratulation, if not euphoria, swept through the black community. "That made a lasting impression on me," one student at Avery testified. "It convinced me that things can change when black people organize."

Clark no doubt had that episode in mind when thinking of ways to challenge the anti-NAACP statute of 1956. When she lost her job, she was in a sense free. She had gotten married in 1920 to a sailor, Nerie Clark, but he died of kidney failure five years after their wedding, and their son, Nerie Jr., was raised by his family. "I never married again," said Clark. "Never had the feeling that I wanted to." She lived in a house on Charleston's Henrietta Street, one she had purchased in 1948, having saved most of her salary for three decades. The specter of loneliness is never far away when you consider any part of her life, though unbound as she was, she could set her own schedule and enlist in as many local affairs as she liked; teaching, for her, was never enough, and "with the exception of the NAACP," wrote Clark biographer Katherine Mellen Charron, "Clark's civic activism continued to express itself in woman-centered organizations, and she became well known among the cadre of black women busy in both communal and interracial social welfare work."

It was through this kind of civic and welfare work that Clark learned of the Highlander Folk School in Monteagle, Tennessee, when the director of a Charleston YWCA suggested she accompany her on a trip there. Close to the mountains, in coal miner country, Highlander had been founded in 1932 and was directed by Myles Horton, a man of the left who had studied with Reinhold Niebuhr at Union Theological Seminary in New York and traveled to Denmark to observe the customs of their folk schools. Highlander had traditionally been devoted to union organizing, yet as the 1950s wore on, it turned more of its attention to race, hosting workshops that invited people from across America, black and white, to discuss the realities of effecting integration. Southern aristocrats—newspapermen, governors, and legislators—harbored a fixation with the place, believing it to be overrun with communists and bent on miscegenation. In the months before Clark visited the school for the first time—in the summer of 1954—James Eastland, a senator from Mississippi, opened a federal investigation into Highlander's practices.

Clark liked the rustic atmosphere of Monteagle and its view of the Cumberland range, though Highlander's way of doing things shocked her at first. "I was surprised," she said, "to know that white women would sleep in the same room that I slept in, and it was really strange, very much so, to be eating at the same table with them." Clark wrote two brochures during that visit, one titled *A Guide to Community Action for Public School Integration*, and when she returned to Monteagle two months later, she brought a resident of Johns Island with her. Esau Jenkins belonged to the executive committee of Charleston's NAACP chapter, and he had known Clark since he was a boy. He drove a bus into the city each morning, carrying longshoremen and domestics and factory workers as well as goods to be sold at market. Jenkins was savvy, a bit of a schemer, and he understood more clearly than most the need of gaining entry into local politics. He had run for school board and narrowly lost, and when he visited Highlander he related the following story: One morning Alice Wine, who was a regular passenger on his bus, said she wanted to register to vote. But she could not read, and the South Carolina application had a literacy requirement; one had to recite a passage of the state constitution. Jenkins obtained a copy of the form and helped Wine learn the words. She memorized the passage and was added to the list of eligible voters. Elated by the event, she asked Jenkins if there was a place on Johns Island where she might formally learn how to read. There was not.

"This is not going to happen with everybody," said Jenkins at Highlander, "and it's important for us to get our people registered. I need a school. I need somebody to help me. Tell me *how* I can get a school going to teach my people."

Not long ago I visited Abraham Jenkins, Esau's son. He lives in Charleston, is in his eighties and looks faintly like his father, or like the pictures I've seen of his father. The lips are set in the same way and his eyes are slightly hooded, as Esau's were. We drove around Johns Island on a Monday in February. It was snowing inland, though here, along the coastal islands, there was just a strong wind and chill rain. We made the turn onto River Road and passed Moving Star Hall, site of the all-night shouts. Its name had changed to something else, and the former austerity of the place was no more. The floors were carpeted, and the rows of wooden benches had been removed. Now, on days when the church opened its doors, contemporary gospel was sung, with an organ and drums and guitar. The customs of the old praise house had been lost, even while the building was still standing and serving as an emblem of sorts, a monument to the old world. It is hard for things to disappear in the South, I reflected. Everything goes on, transmuted maybe—but still enduring. Sitting blankly among the flats, Moving Star Hall was a curio of the landscape, like the hollowed-out pump station one passes on country roads, with its bygone lettering still visible, or the kudzu-infested houses, the vines growing out and around the warped boards.

From my side of the car you could see acres of farmable land trailing away in the distance, and I asked Abraham Jenkins if cotton was what was planted in these fields when he was a boy. "Everybody used to plant cotton," he said, "but you couldn't make no money off cotton, especially black folk. Cotton is one of those crops that it takes so long from the time you plant it to harvest; you couldn't do just cotton and make any money off it unless you were one of those big farmers. When you pull all those seeds out of it, cotton so light, you didn't have no money."

Esau owned a modest piece of land, three acres. "He had collard greens, cabbage, potato, white potato, mustard, and carrot," said Abraham Jenkins. "That was basically what he used to plant. Then when he got to the market—let me tell you how he started buying and selling out of the market. His mother died when he was about eight years old. His father remarried, and the person his father remarried to had two sons. In his estimation he was getting all the hard work, what with the other two sons; he used to live with a lady across the street, and he stayed until he got about twelve or thirteen and left and started working on a boat in the city. He was a deckhand, and after he cleaned the deck he used to go downstairs with the motorman, the man that keep the engine trim, and this guy was a Greek. They start speaking a little bit, and he went to a school that was teaching some Greek to the black folks, and it got that he could speak a little.

"One day they said he couldn't go out because the weather was bad. My daddy and some more went to the market, right across the street from where the potato boats were coming in. This lady had a bushel of plum, asked him, 'Why don't you buy this bushel of plum and I'll give you this little quart to measure it with and you can sell it by the quart while you're waiting in the market?' She had a doctor's appointment. He must have paid seventy-five cents for that bushel of plum. People come up and pay fifteen or twenty cents for a quart. He made more for that bushel of plum than he made for a day on the boat. So he started hustling out of the market. Greeks had most of the corner stores in Charleston then. So he started getting orders from them, and when he started getting orders from them, he figured: 'Why do you all want to come down here and buy stuff off the market when you could give me your order and I could drop it off to your store?' He would get more orders than he could afford, so he bought an old Ford truck. He started coming out here, buying some of his daddy's food, going to other places, buying stuff off the field. Plus what he had, he could make two, three loads a day. And that's when people started riding the truck to go to work in the morning. From that he went from the truck business to the bus business."

A classically American story, you might say. It has all the elements, the grieving boy scorned by his stepmother who leaves home, experiences seafaring and adventure, and through his own pluck earns fortune and respect. A fable in the Horatio Alger mode, except as an African American in the South, Jenkins could never be like Alger's Ragged Dick, never open a shop on Main Street or become heir to an industry, endowed with membership in a country club and all the trappings of bourgeois life. The wealth in this strain of rags-to-riches was not an empire of money but a school, a way to initiate the members of a community into the basic entitlements of democracy.

Myles Horton had visited Johns Island, and he knew a school for adults could work there so long as it was held in wintertime, during breaks between the harvest and planting seasons. He loaned Esau Jenkins $1,500 of Highlander's money to buy an abandoned school on River Road. Jenkins named it the Progressive Club and converted the front room to a store, offering tobacco for sale as well as fruit and other necessaries, and using the profits to pay back the loan. Clark recorded her plans for the class in a series of memoranda titled "Education for Citizenship," and the final detail to be negotiated was perhaps the most critical: who would the teacher be? Clark was unavailable. She had accepted a job as Highlander's Director of Education, which obliged her to live in Monteagle during the winter and to go out on the occasional fundraising tour. She and Horton did not want a trained teacher anyway—the age of the students and their inevitable unease in such a setting, they thought, would require someone effacing, without a reliance on traditional methods.

They approached Bernice Robinson, Clark's cousin. She owned a beauty salon in Charleston, served as membership chair of the local NAACP, and had also participated in Highlander workshops. She had been in attendance when Jenkins put out his call for the school, and though she was somewhat worldly—had lived in New York City for years and been involved in political campaigns there—his speech struck her with the force of revelation. "I knew that there was a lot of illiteracy all around me," Robinson later commented, "but I accepted that as a fact. That was gonna be there, you know, and there was nothing anybody could do about it. But when Esau started talking, I thought, 'Yeah, that *is* something to think about. People can't read.'"

Robinson demurred at first, as she did not feel qualified to teach, but in the end she accepted, and the first meeting in the Progressive Club took place on Monday, January 7, 1957. There were fourteen students, ten women and four men. Robinson brought some teaching aids given to her by her sisters-in-law, who taught in the elementary grades, but quickly realized those materials would be worthless, "too juvenile," as she later said. "I just had to reach them on their level." The class met for two hours twice a week. No outsider could guess what was transpiring in the backrooms of the Progressive Club, and the activity would not have appeared subversive anyway, but more like a club meeting, spearheaded by a beautician gifted in badinage. Students brought their children to class. Robinson taught the younger ones how to crochet, and when it came to literacy she employed a variety of methods. She matched words with pictures, diagrammed syllables, and unwittingly repeated a technique Clark had employed on the island four decades earlier: she asked her students to relate a story, copied it out and read it back to them, isolating certain words. Many of her students brought letters to class—letters they had previously needed whites to read to them—and there were lessons on bank terminology, the policies of a property loan.

If Robinson had reservations at first, that class made her into a teacher for life, and decades later she would recall:

> I can never explain or express how I felt when I put the names of all the students up on the board and I said to this sixty-five-year-old woman, "Now, can you find your name up there on the board?"
>
> "*Yes, ma'am, I sure can.*" She took the ruler out of my hand. "That's my name there, Annie, A-n-n-i-e; and that's my other name down there, Vastine, V-a-s-t-i-n-e." I had goose pimples all over me. That woman could not read or write when she came in that class.

The meetings included more than literacy instruction. A dollar bill, Robinson realized, could illustrate numbers, dollars and cents, units of ten. She traced a money order on onionskin and handed out copies, explaining how to fill them in. The students also scanned newspaper advertisements, budgeted grocery lists, and placed sample orders in the Sears and Roebuck catalog.

Clark had been away on a fundraising tour for most of January, and was unable to observe Robinson's technique until it was almost the course's final week. "I had her teach the session that night, because I wanted to see whether her approach was anything similar to mine," Robinson said. "To my surprise she presented the lessons in the same manner as I had been doing. I had written on the blackboard those difficult and unusual words found on the application blank for voter registration, supplied the definitions of each so that the students would understand what they were reading, also breaking them down in syllables for easier pronunciation."

Those difficult words may have been "fornication" or "larceny," which were listed among the various crimes each applicant had to attest to having never been convicted of, or they could have been "elector" and "certify," the sort that belong in a registrar's argot. The South Carolina application in those days consisted of a single page, and for Robinson's class the clause in question was the fourth. It read, "I will demonstrate to the Registration board that (a) I can both read and write a section of the Constitution of South Carolina; or (b) I own and have paid all taxes last year on property in this State assessed at $300.00 or more."

(B), one feels, could be utilized as a safety hatch for illiterate whites who might own more property than a poor black farmer. It was easier, at any rate, to register in South Carolina in those days than in other parts of the Deep South. In Alabama and Mississippi, one could read and still not be approved, for one would also be asked to interpret a passage to the satisfaction of the registrar, a mug's game. But when Robinson's class adjourned in February, eight of the fourteen students registered immediately. Horton decided the program would continue, and the class picked up more students in December 1957. Two months later, the remaining six from the first group were approved as voters, as were several more. In 1958 courses began on Wadmalaw and Edisto Islands, and the following year one was hosted in North Charleston. All across the Low Country, African Americans began registering to vote.

Clark eventually created a textbook of sorts, called *My Reading Booklet*, made of eighteen mimeographed sheets, containing a map of the United States and of Charleston and a copy of the voter application; its chapters explained the purpose of political parties, how to pay state and federal taxes, what social security was, how to fill in money orders, and provided a list of clinics offering health care. In later editions Clark added this introductory note: "The citizenship schools are for adults. The immediate program is literacy. It enables students to pass literacy tests for voting. But there is involved in the mechanics of learning to read and write an all-round education in community development which includes housing, recreation, health and improved home life."

If Clark understood the totality of literacy training, she also realized that in this context education counted as a political act, and it was the achievement of her life to spread that vision throughout the South. Without dismissing the talents of Jenkins, Horton, and Robinson, it is possible to view the schools as an extension of her personality, meshing education with activism.

When approaching this subject, one runs up against the limits of the historical imagination. It is difficult in the present day to understand how far removed Johns Islanders were from the mainstream political process. Many African Americans across the South came of age in the early and mid-twentieth century without an awareness of the political structures of our country; the sacred documents of American democracy were not always a point of emphasis in black schools of the Jim Crow era. To teach someone how to vote, then, entailed more than enabling them to read a paragraph and sign a name; it was like giving a tutorial on another nation, an exotic land—except the state in question was not an exotic land, but rather one's own polity.

Among the papers Robinson distributed to her students, for instance, was one titled "Constitutional Amendments." On the top a paragraph described the Bill of Rights. Below that, Section I of the Fourteenth Amendment was written out in full. Evidently no other amendment received its own sheet. The article that mattered most, in other words, was not the one securing freedom of worship or the right to bear arms but equal protection under the law. Four paragraphs of annotation accompany the text of Section I. They begin, "The purpose of this amendment was to grant citizenship to the newly freed Negro slaves, to extend to them full civil rights." Going on, the explanatory passage describes how, until 1954 and *Brown*, equal protection was held to be compatible with segregation. Anyone who studied this sheet would be introduced simultaneously to the law and to its selective enforcement, and could infer that for some, rights would only be enjoyed with maximum vigilance. In these citizenship classes, it would seem, a naturalization into our democratic system also meant a naturalization into the movement.

As their number grew, the classes were bound to garner the attention of the white community, and they became subject of a series of articles published in the spring of 1959 by Thomas Waring, editor of the Charleston *News and Courier*. Highlander, that point of fascination for Southern lawmen, was raided not long after; in July 1959 police showed up in Monteagle bearing a search warrant, claiming suspicion that alcohol was being served in a dry county. Septima Clark was arrested for an unstated charge to begin with, though after a few bottles of rum and gin as well as a cask were found in Myles Horton's lodgings, the crime was listed as illegal possession and sale of whiskey. The allegation was later dropped, but under examination some months later, Horton admitted to serving beer at his workshops, and a jury found him guilty of using the school for personal gain, a paltry charge: in 1957 the house he stayed in and seventy acres of land had been transferred to his name, in recognition of the fact that he had never drawn a salary in all the years he served as Highlander's director. But the school's charter was revoked in February 1960, and Tennessee's Supreme Court upheld the ruling.

In 1961, then, operation of the citizenship schools shifted to Martin Luther King's organization, the Southern Christian Leadership Conference. Horton acknowledged that was bound to happen anyway. "We weren't interested in administering a running program," he said. "We were just interested in developing it." Clark and Robinson joined the staff of the SCLC, who had other personnel in line—Dorothy Cotton, Andrew Young, Annell Ponder—to implement the Citizenship Education Program, as it was called. Students were found through word of mouth. Cotton, Young, or Clark would follow up on a call or letter that had come in to the SCLC offices, and one of them would drive to a church or some other prearranged meeting spot and describe what participants could expect to learn from the class.

The SCLC's clout and financial backing were greater than Highlander's had been, which meant the scope of the project would be enlarged significantly. Workshops to train a cadre of teachers were held at the Dorchester Academy, a former school for freedmen in McIntosh, Georgia. They lasted five days and were normally attended by fifty or sixty people. The emphasis was more explicitly political than it had been on Johns Island; some discussions focused on coalition building, for instance. "We wanted to make the basic documents on which our country—yes, *our country*—is founded come alive," Cotton wrote about the trainings in Georgia. "We wanted them to see themselves no longer simply as 'consumers' of government, but rather to see the government as 'us.'" Attendees of one class would recruit for the next, with the aim of creating a dynastic chain, leaders begetting leaders. Between July 1962 and June 1963, close to four hundred attended training and would go on to open classes that enrolled more than five thousand; ultimately those teachers and students would help more than 17,500 people register. A year later, writes Charron in *Freedom's Teacher: The Life of Septima Clark*, there were "more than 50,000 new African American names on southern registration books as a direct result of the program's stimulus."

Other registration drives began concurrently, and often overlapped. Robinson and Ponder were called into the Mississippi Delta in 1963, where the needs were as acute, the health and literacy rates as poor, as what Clark had seen almost half a century before on Johns Island. A school was established. "The classes had not changed much since their early development by Septima Clark and Bernice Robinson," Charles Payne wrote in his study *I've Got The Light of Freedom: The Organizing Tradition and the Mississippi Freedom Struggle*. "Classes met twice a week for three months, concentrating on literacy, the state constitution, and local and state government, but supplementing that with Negro history and community problem-solving, by which they meant boycotts, demonstrations, and the like."

Historically, SNCC's work in Mississippi gets a lot of attention. So does the SCLC's choice to move on Selma, Alabama. The citizenship program as pioneered on Johns Island could be regarded as the ballast or counterpoint to those iconic campaigns. That first class in the Progressive Club remained the model. Most in the movement agreed there was no better way of educating the populace.

In the months following passage of the Voting Rights Act,

Clark visited the counties outside of Selma. The nation's attention was not on voting rights, not anymore. The evening news anchors were no longer there, and neither were Marlon Brando and the other celebrities who jetted into Selma in March of 1965. But Clark was. Not even a decade had passed since she had lost her job for belonging to the NAACP. Legalized segregation was a close memory. So were literacy tests and shifty registrars. The Voting Rights Act had been passed, but the legislation was no good without education to accompany it and set it into action. In the counties surrounding Selma most of the population was African American. Few, if any, had ever voted. Like those on Johns Island, they needed a primer, the farmers and dairymen and domestics, and when they showed up, Clark went to work, teaching them the rudiments of the ballot and how to read and write—how to sign your name, if nothing else, because you cannot inscribe "X" on the bottom of a voter application. No TV crews were present, but one day in Wilcox County a photographer is there to capture the occasion, and the viewfinder shows Clark leaning over a seated man dressed in his Sunday best. She is, too, for that matter, wearing a wool coat buttoned to the knot of a scarf. The light falls over her cropped hair, and she and this man hold the pencil together, and if you want, this is how we can sew it up, the story of the citizenship schools, and bring it to a close, with Clark's hand steering his through the tiny motions needed to bring letters onto the page.

2.

"To me," Septima Clark once said, "social justice is not a matter of money but of will." The citizenship schools are noteworthy not only for the contributions made to registration numbers or the lives of its students. They also serve as a lesson in how to surmount difficulty with the barest resources. The school on Johns Island was a triumph, as Clark said, of will, but also of patience and organization—and duplicable for this reason, which was the point: that the model could be transported. And yet as vast as the program became, almost nobody today knows about the citizenship schools. No mythology adheres to them. Bernice Robinson, Septima Clark: their names are not completely lost to history, but they are not canonical, either, are not as recognizable as the names Martin Luther King or John Lewis.

Documentation is one reason. Robinson's life is difficult to trace in full. The things you need, like letters and video footage and press clippings, are in short supply, meaning it is hard not only to complete the outline but also to balance out the testimony she gave in a handful of oral histories. When you interview those who knew her, the portrait that emerges is more legendary than real, stocked with memory's amplifications. She was a slender and attractive woman and appears taller, in photographs, than the five feet six inches listed on her South Carolina driver's license. Like Clark, Robinson married as a young woman. After her divorce she remained single, and what became of her child, a son, is unknown.

Beyond these facts it's uncertified territory, full of questions and absences, the empty spaces of the past.

During one of my trips to Johns Island I spent a day with the Bernice Robinson papers, which are housed at the College of Charleston. I found her business card. "Glamour Beauty Box 22 Dewey Street," it says at the top, along with its slogan: "If your hair is not becoming to you, you should be coming to us." There were pictures I had never seen before and examples of her handwriting, but how much, really, can you piece together from a person's belongings? The closest I came to feeling like I knew Robinson was when I looked at a sheet of paper that was mostly blank. It was a syllabus for a class, probably the second adult education school, held from December 1957 to February of the following year. "Courses offered: Reading, Writing, Crocheting, Sewing," it said at the top. The slots for two dozen dates were listed below, but other than the first and last and the nights when movies were shown—*The Rural Nurse, Mahatma Gandhi, Walk to Freedom, Of Human Rights, We've Come a Long Long Way*—the line for each class was kept blank. Perhaps she intended to fill it in later, though it is more likely that Robinson knew there was no point in scripting each class. She would adapt to the wants and needs of her students as they expressed themselves.

When we consider Clark, we enter no-man's land again, for in some hallways of academia she is a household name, which gives her a curious distinction, celebrated in the intellectual sphere but omitted from American iconography. There is no movie devoted to her life, no statue that I can think of that has been mounted in her likeness; along with Robinson, she is generally unheard of even among those who have more than a passing understanding of the movement's major events. The citizenship schools are one of those things that get lost in the cracks.

The lack of documentation plays a part, but the chief reason, one suspects, why the schools have not made it into the popular history and folklore is because they are not particularly dramatic. There are no beatings or lynchings, no Molotov cocktail hurled by the Klan at midnight, nothing that might motivate some equivocating Senator to finally cast his lot with the cause of civil rights. If one needs a great tumultuous frieze to hold the eye, here the tapestry is thin, and seems unfinished. What do we see? Robinson standing before a blackboard, charting syllabic patterns. *Not enough*, the writer or screenwriter is apt to conclude.

I remember a comment John Perdew made during our visit in Atlanta. In his mind, the difference between reading about the movement and participating in the movement was considerable. "Authors," he said, "think the civil rights movement happened only when there were pickets and demonstrations, which is a farce. I realize that authors need to be dramatic, but I wish there was more about the day-to-day activity involved in building a movement, the day-to-day, unglamorous activity."

But how does one relate day-to-day, unglamorous activity? You can do it, but only in shorthand. "Days passed"; "Movement leaders hunkered down for weeks of strategizing"; "They canvassed door-to-door, meeting with the town's citizens, the hours long, grueling, and uneventful." For a writer, day-to-day activity is a stopgap, a way of marking time. It doesn't sustain attention, and it does not excite the passions, to call on Aristotle's definition of drama.

Which brings us to another curious distinction Septima Clark holds in movement history: she is the dedicatee of *Parting the Waters*, the first volume of Taylor Branch's trilogy *America in the King Years*, even though of the trilogy's 2,300 pages no more than a handful are devoted to Clark, and there is not a single mention of the school on Johns Island. The trilogy is laudable and exemplary in several respects, yet Branch is well aware of the shortcomings of his tale; he knows that inevitably some things were left out. "*Parting the Waters* is dedicated to the late Septima Clark for a peculiar reason," he wrote recently. "Interviews with her left a strong personal effect on me, confirming what others from the civil rights movement felt, but she had functioned almost entirely 'offstage' from the main historical narrative, as it were, teaching literacy and citizenship to rural sharecroppers. My gesture was a personal gesture of tribute mixed with regret, because I found it impossible within my storytelling rules to include Septima Clark in proportion to her influence."

What Branch is saying is that history is one thing, and the story another. "Main historical narrative" seems like an objectionable phrase, and it raises the question of how one decides what is "main" and what is not. But the fact is, there are certain things you must have in order to make a story, and if you begin to catalog a few of those needs and examine how history can be bent and molded in such a way as to fulfill them, you inch closer to an understanding of the sobering implications of Branch's comment, which is that if you drop out of the narrative, you drop out of history.

Shape is one of those needs, since one of the major functions of story is to provide form and definition to the morass of experience. Imagine that you have been assigned the task of writing a brief yet somewhat detailed account of the civil rights movement, for public television perhaps, or for a pamphlet accompanying a museum display. Montgomery, Alabama, provides an unavoidable starting point, not only because the bus boycott marked the beginning of Martin Luther King's rise as a public figure, but also because the story will unwind in such a way as to return there, with a nice round number, a decade, elapsing in between. When Rosa Parks stood up in Montgomery in 1955, the movement began, and ten years later it came home again, after much ordeal and bloodshed, though now with a president's blessing and the right of the franchise secured. Rosa Parks was on hand for the conclusion of the march from Selma to Montgomery in 1965. She stood at the podium that had been placed on the steps of the state capitol, and we are invited to picture her looking out at the marchers, a sea of thousands, and reflecting on all she had engendered. What competent writer could refuse this touch? Or forget to point out that Montgomery had also been named the original capital of the Confederacy in 1861? And a century after, during his swearing-in as governor, George Wallace stood on the same steps where Jefferson Davis had taken his oath and promised the citizens of Alabama "segregation now, segregation tomorrow, segregation forever." When King mounted those steps at the end of the Selma march, it was like a conqueror entering the residence of his warring counterpart, a president or general, and flying a new flag overhead.

Now the outline is in place, the beginning and end joined in such a way as to make a round and felicitous shape. The middle must be filled with suspense. There should be setback, a give-and-take; readers might have a sense the story tends back to the beginning, but they must not believe it to be foreordained. Otherwise they will feel no relief once the battle is won. Here history readily accommodates, and does not need to be adjusted all that much. Selma helps, too, by winding things to the maximum torque and bringing our story to the point where all must either collapse or consummate. In Alabama in 1965 the separate factions of the movement are at odds; SNCC has lost patience with King and his alleged grandstanding; then Bloody Sunday happens, forcing the president to declare himself once and for all. And before a joint session of Congress Johnson quotes "We Shall Overcome" and announces legislation—the Voting Rights Act—that the movement has been lobbying for and dying for. Later he orders military protection for the march from Selma to Montgomery. That march will begin at a bridge, the Edmund Pettus Bridge that arches over the Alabama River, and in a sense we will all be crossing over, into a new America, free of the cancer of segregation and racial strife.

"Then after that the children of Israel journeyed," reports Numbers in the Old Testament, "and in the place where the cloud abode, there the children of Israel pitched their tents." The march from Selma to Montgomery, which was punctuated by rain, and stretched out over days along a road adjoining cotton and soy fields emerging from the rawness of winter, seems a modern retelling of this journey, and it is not alone, for many episodes in movement history share the lineaments of mythology. The movement's epic shape is due in part to the way it harkens back to the epics of the past, linking arms with the most beloved archetypes and tales and merging seamlessly with Biblical and American legend. Think of the March on Washington. The visual evidence alone, regardless of the "I Have a Dream" speech, teases our mind with layers of pregnant association. We see King standing before the marmoreal gaze of Lincoln, one hundred years after the Emancipation Proclamation, his words ringing out before the assembled Israelites. In that single image we summon—and not serially, as read, but together, in a kind of symbolic knot—the idea of King as a modern founding father, writing his own contribution into the history commemorated by the National Mall and siding with the keeper of the Union, the man who, as Moses did, freed the slaves. This is a contradiction, for any freeing of the slaves would obviate the need for a march of this sort, yet it's no matter; the mind rushes on, heedless of the spectacle's larger complexities, its appetite for symbolism and moral instruction overpowering all other considerations.

The March on Washington is one of those things everyone feels comfortable with. For a brief time—from 1963, or maybe earlier, until 1965—the movement was blessed with moral counterbalance, and featured what looks from a distance like perfect good and perfect evil. A story needs that, too. You have people agitating on behalf of a set of claims whose righteousness nobody doubts, and those on the other side, who are trying to hold the line, cannot defend their beliefs without opening themselves up to charges of sanctimony, bigotry, or worse. Large scale, this portrayal is accurate, though only a brief step is required to move from such a summary into straw-figure land, where the members of an entire region, the South, or indeed all of America are banded together in a host of generalities. It is easily forgotten that not all black people marched or not all white people set fire to a cross. Very few know, for instance, that Bull Connor's hoses and dogs not only brought the international community over to King's side during the Birmingham campaign of 1963; they brought the black community to it as well. Till that point, most of the town's black business leaders wished that King—who was not a resident of Birmingham and would not be around to reap the consequences of what he wrought—would go away. The demonstrations, in their view, would be a hindrance to racial progress, inciting resistance and setting the African American struggle back years.

Details of this kind, the finer points, have no place in the folktale. Inheritance and tradition—the most exacting editor of any— will winnow them out until everything is clear-cut and can be told quickly. It is good versus evil, and while there will be, as noted, a give-and-tug throughout the course of the drama, we really have no interest in seeing the inner workings of the competing armies. The struggle is what matters, though a terrible question awaits us once that struggle has exhausted itself, which is: when does good cease to be good? After Selma the movement is no longer a crusade. How can it be, when both integration and voting rights have been won? Many of its leaders oppose the Vietnam War, believing nonviolence should extend into the realm of foreign policy, and they also begin advocating for economic redress to go alongside their newfound political rights. For many Americans this is too much; consensus is lost; and since there is no longer a paragon of virtue set against a paragon of evil, our story ends. The events after Selma must be treated in an epilogue, a tragic denouement that hints at the mixed blessings of victory. Our protagonists have suddenly become upstarts, refusing to acknowledge there is a point beyond which they must not pass. The fight has been won, say the objectors, so why do you keep on fighting?

Nevertheless, they do; they keep on fighting until the moment when their vatic figure, King, is lost, at which point our story has reached the last page and the cover can be closed. In movement lore, there are more than enough heroes to go around, and there are colorful villains and high-ranking villains, but there is only one prophet. On every score save the extramarital affairs, King was too pure and virtuous for this world. "I refuse to hate," he said, and there is nothing in the public record to rebut such an assertion. The apostle of nonviolence, he led his people out of bondage, a feat for which the ultimate price must be exacted, and was. What is more, he knew about this fate, was martyred a day after predicting it. "Like anybody I would like to live a long life," he said in Memphis on the night of April 3, 1968, before moving toward what amounted to his last public words, which offered both the promise of salvation and a foreshadowing of his own death: "I've seen the promised land. I may not get there with you. But I want you to know tonight, that we, as a people, will get to the promised land."

The speech was improvised. King had a cold that night and tried to beg out of his speaking obligation, sending his top lieutenant, Ralph Abernathy, to the meeting to preach in his place. But too many people showed up, so King went over at the last minute, and the fact that he chose to ruminate on the inevitability of his own death not twenty-four hours before he was slain at the Lorraine Motel allows people to reconcile themselves to the murder, to make peace with it. He knew it was coming, they say. Even those who, like Andrew Young, another SCLC aide, were near him when the shot came, will say this. Recently I heard Young remark in a documentary about the Memphis strike that King had done his work, that it was time to go.

If you stand on the spot where King was killed, which I did not long ago, you look out over the short rise of a hill and through some trees to the window from which the rifle emerged. A memorial plaque rests on the ground floor below; tourists are constantly taking pictures, and a slab of cement lighter in shade than what surrounds it indicates where the pool of blood was and the floor had to be replaced. Pretty much the last thing that comes to mind during such an experience is that it was all meant to be. From up there the odds that the murder attempt would fail seem pretty good—the angle, the timing—and an immense weariness sets in, for King's death, while obviously tragic, was probably even more tragic, if there is room for the needle to go higher, because of the fact that it occurred at the start of the Poor People's Campaign,* which he thought of as his last and central mission. There was never any plan to go to Memphis. When the garbage workers' strike gained wider attention, all of his associates and allies except one—James Lawson—told him to stay away. But he went anyhow, against counsel, against pragmatism, and that was the choice for which he died.

Again, out come the Biblical allusions and precedents. Abernathy cited Genesis when giving the eulogy for his fallen friend and comrade: "Behold, here cometh the Dreamer . . . let us slay him, and we will see what becomes of his dreams." Even Taylor Branch, who is writing history, which we normally think of as a materialist or objective field, resorts to otherworldly rhetoric when depicting the assassination. "King stood still for once," he writes of the moment when the shot rang out, "and his sojourn on earth went blank." King, we are led to infer, was an emissary from another world and destined to be in our midst for just a short span. His life was a temporary visitation, a "sojourn," and his death was

---

* An initiative launched by the Southern Christian Leadership Conference in 1968 to combat poverty and its associated ills. The Poor People's Campaign recruited members of several races and extraction, and its activities were geared toward, among other things, pressuring Congress to pass an economic bill of rights.

thus not a death but only a completion of that visit, after which he might return to the holy ethereality from whence he came.

The psychology motivating this viewpoint is fairly easy to understand, and can be described as compensatory; so great was the loss of King that the only way to live with it is to make his murder seem an act of predestination. So we wrap it up, place the incident in a numinous shroud, and hope it turns into something else, something sensible or beatific. He did not die in vain, we say, because stories, even the tragic ones, must be purposive, and point us toward some truth, moral, or lesson. And there is no purpose, no quest or outcome, quite like freedom. As King said in that last speech on April 3: "Wherever they are assembled today, whether they are in Johannesburg, South Africa; Nairobi, Kenya; Accra, Ghana; New York City; Atlanta, Georgia; Jackson, Mississippi; or Memphis, Tennessee, the cry is always the same: 'We want to be free.'"

Chop the civil rights movement in this way and it makes for the greatest story ever told. That sentence is not intended ironically. It scratches every available itch, moral, philosophical, and dramatic, has a clear beginning, middle, and end, and that tripartite structure includes the expression and focusing of a problem and the arrival at some sort of solution.

Once you understand the appeal of what might be called the common or Ur-narrative of the movement, and realize how much that story shapes our view of the struggle, then a lot of other things fall into place—the patriarchal emphasis, for example. Has the civil rights movement been led by men? No, but the most dramatic protests have. The demonstrations in Selma and Birmingham were overseen by ministers, with the church handling recruitment and protocol, staging meetings and workshops, and it would be difficult to imagine an environment more stubbornly masculine than Baptist churches in the South in the last century, though sexism is not a regional phenomenon, of course. Women were also relegated to the background of the March on Washington, and half the constituency of that event derived from labor communities in the North. In truth, there have always been two strains of the civil rights movement, complementary ones. Demonstration, or nonviolent disobedience of law, accounts for one, and organizing, the kind of work that can hide in plain sight, since meeting in a cooperative store does not appear on the face of it to be scandalous, counts as another. Martin Luther King, Ralph Abernathy, and other ministers in the Southern Christian Leadership Conference marched, while Septima Clark, Bernice Robinson, and Dorothy Cotton ran the Citizenship Education Program. One might venture that women make better organizers because they are at the root of the family structure and can thus reach into a community with greater ease—but this is a dangerous contention, and really no gender is naturally predisposed to one type of work more than the other. Look at Esau Jenkins. He was just about the best organizer you could imagine.

Poll a hundred Americans, though, and ask for a definition of the civil rights movement, and you will not get two strains. You will get one. Organizing, as John Perdew remarked, is not particularly glamorous, and is excluded from popular memory. When Julian Bond says the fiftieth anniversaries of events like the March on Washington and Freedom Summer serve to remind him "of how little we know," he doubtless refers, in part, to our imperfect cultural memory. Everything about a demonstration is defined and clear; as Bayard Rustin said, that is one of its appeals, its primary purpose. It takes place at a specific time in a specific location, and its aims are spelled out on poster boards. A reaction is provoked immediately or it is not, and the success of the endeavor therefore seems easy to gauge.

Organizing, on the other hand, is glacial, unfixed, a compound of meetings and interactions spanning several years across a region, and given these traits—its amorphousness and undramatic character—it can't help but get lost, for generally it offers nothing for the popular imagination to seize on.

"Those moments," Maisha Moses said when we were talking of the sixties, about the March on Washington and the most famous protests, "happen because they stand on years and years and years of work and organizing and most of it hidden." Too much, you might say, to fit into a single frame, and ideally, when we look at a moment like the March on Washington we would also be able to see, behind or beneath it, like a palimpsest that bears the hand of generations, the hundreds or thousands of other moments that inhere in that one. But that we cannot do.

And so, this raises an essential question: if the civil rights movement is not something we typically see as a living phenomenon, an ongoing or continuous presence, is that because of the lack of a current movement or due to our habits of seeing?

PART THREE

Forward Together

I.

The Mississippi Delta, an alluvial plain in the northwest part of the state of Mississippi, extends south from Memphis to Vicksburg, where the Mississippi and Yazoo Rivers cross. It was the flooding of those rivers, year after year, that created the Delta as we know it, the water stocking the soil with nutrients and creating a land of uncommon fertility. Delta topsoil was the original black gold, and that brought the planters, who instituted a system of sharecropping, whereby whites would own the plantations and blacks would tend to them, ostensibly for a piece of the profits, but with the planter exacting rent and money for supplies, often arbitrarily and at high interest rates, a sharecropper usually never retired the debt but was only driven further into it. In the earliest years of the twentieth century, though, before it was widely accepted that the game was fixed, African Americans needed jobs and moved into the region by the tens of thousands. Before the Great Migration, there was another great migration, only this one led into the Delta, not out of it.

For tourists and Mississippians alike, the Delta is a source of myth. It has been called the most brutal region in America, the poorest and most backward, but also the most American, as though one has something to do with the other, and to be the epitome of America you must strip away all comfort and illusion. That's what the Delta is, a stripping away. You can see that as you drive south on Highway 61, through the old swamp and forestlands that were clear-cut after the Choctaws and other native tribes were removed west. The land starts to open up, an infinite expanse, one field after another stretching into the haze beyond. The horizon is so vast that storms can be spotted hours before they arrive, and the weather patterns quarter the sky, arraying it in different shades of blue. Clear to the east, and pelting rain to the west.

Life is not easy here. The Delta is the poorest part of Mississippi, and Mississippi is the poorest part of the United States. The health care and education statistics are uniformly grim. The Delta is dying, it is said, but it has been dying for a long time now, and one gets the sense that its decay is as infinite as the fields turning out endlessly, and that there will be no final expiration. Not far from Clarksdale, a marker identifies one of the fields as belonging to the Hopson plantation, where cotton picking was mechanized in 1944. It is tempting to view this plaque as the Delta's epitaph, for the new machine could do the whole job on its own, from planting to harvest, and that meant even if the wrongs of sharecropping were magically corrected there would still be a surplus of labor.

But the truth is the Delta was always doomed, and could never subsist on its own. During the segregation battles of the 1960s, Mississippi's senior senator, James Eastland, the owner of a large plantation in Sunflower County—and the one who had pressed for an investigation into the Highlander Folk School—collected millions in federal subsidies for his farm while advocating for interposition and insisting the federal government had no place in the state's affairs. That tradition carries on today, the farming, the handouts. Mississippi continues to receive more aid from Washington than any other state while resisting "federal intervention" in voting and other affairs.

———

Clarksdale is not only home of the Hopson Plantation, it is also where Highway 49 intersects with 61, creating the crossroads of blues mythology. Many visit the town and try to envision Robert Johnson selling his soul to the devil, although the vision is difficult to realize at the present crossroads, a busy and built-up thoroughfare, with auto repair shops and junk shops gathered around the stoplight. Highway 61 has been moved east twice since Johnson's lifetime. However, the old downtown that lies a mile beyond is a different story. This is a site hollowed out and bare, a mausoleum of itself. The empty lodgings and storefronts, the signs left in the cracked display windows or under drapes that haven't budged in decades: it all gives the sense that one has stumbled onto a private Pompeii recently uncovered, and confirms the notion of the Delta as a place that is battered and beyond time, the shale out of which peeled this strangely beautiful exfoliation, the blues.

Blight, in other words, is an essential feature of the myth, but Clarksdale is not something to be romanticized. The drug trade is active, for as easy as it is in Mississippi to acquire guns, a pipeline has been established, with arms going north to Chicago in exchange for heroin and cocaine. Poverty and unemployment are systemic, and while to the tourist's eyes the empty buildings may be evocative, they are a symbol, ultimately, of indolence. One afternoon, as I drove through downtown, in part simply to drive and in part to see if the blues club Morgan Freeman opened had attracted any more businesses—it had not—I wondered what would happen if a news crew came to Clarksdale, filmed for a day and then aired a story, only labeling it as set in Uganda or the Central African Republic or some other foreign place. Would the story go viral and become a cause célèbre, with donations pouring in from New York and California? It is such a curious thing, what excites our outrage, and I suppose it all depends on what we've become adjusted to. The crumpled houses in Clarksdale, the slum rows: in many areas of the Deep South, I thought, such conditions are routine and familiar and less apt, therefore, to strike us as abject.

Only this is not quite right, because the Delta *is* a cause célèbre, one of the most studied places on the planet. Every ten minutes, it seems, somebody publishes a dissertation about the Delta, its history or economy, and for the past fifty years people have been streaming in, determined to effect some kind of change, be it charities like the Kellogg Foundation or luminaries such as Robert Kennedy, who passed through in 1967 and later made hunger a major item of his political agenda. King visited the Delta the following year, near the end of his life; he traveled to Marks, half an hour east of Clarksdale, and saw the poverty, which was like nothing he had encountered before, not even in the ghettoes of Chicago. He spoke in a church whose walls were made of calendars, and when he saw a mother splitting open an apple and dividing it into fourths to feed her children, he began to cry, and resolved to start a caravan in Marks, a legion of the poor to march from Mississippi to Washington, D.C. Today a sign nailed to a tree outside the town limits commemorates that choice. WELCOME TO MARKS HOME OF THE MULE TRAIN, it says in reference to the mule-drawn wagons and carts that made up the parade, which left the Delta a little more than a month after King's assassination, in May of 1968.

But the Delta is stubborn and follows its own course and logic more than the design of any outside agency—progress or technological advancement seems to go around rather than through it. And there's always another level; just when you think you've reached the bottom you realize you haven't. Jessie Tyler has lived in Ruleville in Sunflower County all her life, not far from Senator Eastman's old plantation, and yet she never knew how bad the Delta was, she said, until she gathered statistics for the census in 2000 and again in 2010.

"Out in the fields was when I really discovered," she told me.

"People didn't even have running water, and I didn't know this kind of stuff still existed, in this day and age? That's what made me go back in 2010. This time I branched out and worked LeFlore and Tallahatchie, to see if things had changed. Well, it was worse than Sunflower County, and I'm like, Good Lord Jesus. It was real bad in Tallahatchie. Some houses you went to, a two-bedroom house, you got fifteen people staying there. Tallahatchie seemed to have more people that wasn't working. They had no kind of income, and I couldn't even picture no income. How do you live in this day and time with no income?"

We were driving near the fields surrounding Ruleville, on choppy gravel roads next to tufts of soybean and stalks of wheat shifting lazily in the wind. I stopped outside what was plainly a school, seeing the low-lying building, the twin rows of horizontal windows across each floor, and the parking lot abutting the football field. Only there was something sinister about this school. On the side of a shed close to the football field the Confederate flag was painted brightly. Another relic, I thought, yet another example, the thousandth or ten thousandth I had seen, of time standing still in the South, and I was about to ask how long this school had stood abandoned when Tyler cut in, "That's the private school. Sunflower County School, a white school. They got one black that's enrolled there now. They finally let in one. I told my husband I wanted our daughter to go out there because I wanted to see would they let her in, but he was so strongly against me sending her out there, I just wouldn't."

Tyler is in her late forties and heavyset. Her accent is thick and musical, the stresses in her speech so decisive that, if you wanted, you could break certain sentences down in poetic feet. At night she works as a guard at the Parchman farm prison, the most notorious of American penitentiaries. Like Alcatraz, they say you cannot escape from it. The features of the Delta landscape, the breadth of land without cover, prevent it, making escapees easy to spot if the heat does not attenuate their physical powers first.* Tyler has worked at Parchman since she graduated from Tougaloo College in Jackson. It was important to her parents that she attend college, she said: "My daddy always wanted us to never struggle with anything. He said when he was coming up he used to run track with Jesse Owens; he said he was faster than Jesse Owens but his mama couldn't afford to send him to track and he was never able to compete, and he never wanted that for his child, didn't want them to miss out on opportunities."

And so her family had what many families have and require if they are to step outside their caste: an animating myth, an image to act either against or in allegiance to. As a result Tyler was spared the trapdoors of the Delta, an incomplete education and sporadic employment, yet as shocked as she was to discover what living conditions are like in her native area, she chooses to go into that territory again and again. She not only volunteered for the census twice, but works by day to help those who previously could not purchase health insurance to sign up for a plan using the marketplace created by the Affordable Care Act. Every Sunday Tyler sits in a room at her church, at a spare desk, and escorts someone through the enrollment process, which can last as long as two hours. On the other days of the week she is in her car, driving the back roads of Sunflower, Tallahatchie, LeFlore, and Bolivar Counties. Many residents of those counties, even if they qualify for health insurance, have no way of getting to Tyler. Transportation is one of the Delta's scarcities—transportation and access to the internet. Tyler carries a hotspot with her on days when she is doing fieldwork, driving out to the sort of homes we were passing now, dingy and busted up. The porch of one had completely

---

* As if in proof of this axiom there is no perimeter around Parchman, no wall to mark the limits of the property—just the bare acreage and the heat, the Delta's elemental defenses.

given way and was spilling its debris—splintered wood, collapsed tiles—onto an old and soiled trailer that stood next door.

"You get houses like this stacked up on one another when you get in rural-rural areas," she said, and then, a little lower: "You getting a feel for the quality of life around here now ain't you?" This was stated without irony. And there were times that afternoon when we seemed to step outside America, and I had the slightly languid, tentative feeling one gets in a foreign country. You cannot take anything for granted in the Delta; your assumptions and habits, all your old knowledge, none of them are any good here.

―――――

Tyler's official title is health navigator. She is not a doctor or nurse, not a trained medical practitioner, more like a liaison. She understands the byzantine system of American health care, the endless complications, the way one seemingly innocuous detail can alter the overall picture. It is her job to take all that complication and render it in ordinary human language.

She is by no means the only navigator in the state, but is part of a network, five dozen in number, led by Michael Minor, the pastor of Oak Hill Missionary Baptist Church in Hernando, Mississippi. Minor is known for his advocacy of healthy living. After being appointed pastor in 1996, he dubbed Oak Hill a "no fry zone," barring the Southern staple of fried chicken from church outings, and he created a "walking track" around Oak Hill, not a track per se but a measurement, seven and a half times around the church equaling one mile. After service Minor will walk laps with his congregation. These efforts earned him the attention of the media—Minor has been written about in the *New York Times* and Reuters—as well as an audience with Michelle Obama. He helped other churches coordinate anti-obesity campaigns, and when the federal government announced they would be awarding "navigator grants" in the months leading up to the first enrollment period of the Affordable Care Act, Oak Hill successfully applied for one. Only one other grant was given in the state, to the University of Mississippi Medical Center in Jackson. But the hospital announced a policy of only enrolling those patients who had been admitted for care, and knowing that would represent a fraction of Mississippi's uninsured, Minor began to organize, calling ministers around the state and recruiting navigators like Tyler. When enrollment began on October 1, 2013, Minor and his group, called Cover Mississippi, could boast of a navigator planted within an hour's drive of every township in Mississippi. Between that date and the one when the sign-up period ended, March 31, 2014, they had reached some twenty thousand people.

I visited Minor for several reasons, but one of them was because I was hoping to find the legacy of the citizenship schools, a contemporary example of organizing, where similar methods were being used to empower a disadvantaged populace. The story of the citizenship schools ends, you might say, in Wilcox County, Alabama, following passage of the Voting Rights Act, but what about their mission, the beliefs and strategy that undergirded them? They do not end at a specific time or place, and extend well beyond the realms of literacy and education. And that mission and strategy may still be detectable, if we look hard enough. Moral Monday is easy to spot. It has all the flash: the arrests, the swell of the thousands, the galvanizing leader out front. But the organizing that's going on today won't be found on the front page. It would be somewhat hidden, out in those fields where Jessie Tyler knocks on the door of a decrepit trailer with a hotspot in her hand—the kind of activity that goes unreported.

Another reason why organizing is different from marching—and this helps to explain its relative invisibility as well—is that it often means working within the law rather than attempting to change it. It was not illegal in South Carolina in 1958 for an African American to register to vote. There was a series of loopholes and blockages that meant the law was seldom implemented, and the citizenship schools found a way around those blockages, room for maneuver. Which tells us something important: though we regard them as ironclad fixtures of the world around us, a law often exists in a state of potentiality, and does not begin to accrue meaning until some effort is made to enforce it. For laws that extend rights as opposed to those that merely ensure the public safety, the onus falls on the citizen to take advantage of whatever the law was designed to offer. The Affordable Care Act is one such example. People who were formerly denied health coverage can suddenly acquire it. But they have to sign up, and there are plenty of hindrances, some of the workaday sort, like transportation and internet access. Beyond those, a basic misunderstanding persists of what the Affordable Care Act—or Obamacare, as it's often called—really is. The waters have been muddied with propaganda, with rumors of death panels and TV commercials that show Uncle Sam as an invasive gynecologist; in Texas the campaign against Obamacare was so vehement that many in the state—which has more uninsured residents than any other—thought it was illegal to enroll. And many of those signing up have little or no experience with insurance. They don't know what the words "premium" and "deductible" mean, just as those who had never entered a South Carolina courthouse before 1958 did not know what the words "elector" or "larceny" meant.

And yet, for all these parallels, Reverend Minor and his wife Lottie are surprised I would want to travel to Hernando. Their bailiwick is health care, and in Mississippi, they say, "civil rights" means race and the vote. And there is more: the phrase refers to black people, and most of those they have helped to sign up for health insurance are white. Why, if I am writing a book on the civil rights movement, am I coming to see them?

Minor was born in 1965 and raised in Coldwater, Mississippi, a town that is not far from the Memphis commuter path but feels thousands of miles from any urban center. It has the standard look of many Mississippi towns, the four-way stop beside streets of abandoned property, the empty grocery abutting the Dollar Store, which is apt to be the busiest point of commerce on any given day. Minor is of the generation that grew up among the last vestiges of segregation. When he was in high school, two homecoming queens were elected, one white, one black, and during my visit we drove by Coldwater High, a school with an unusual history. When the desegregation mandate came down, the city fathers thought if they made a better school for African Americans then they wouldn't want to integrate, would stay away from the inferior facilities of the white school. Over time the latter fell into disrepair, and eventually the entire student body had to be moved to the newer structure, the one originally intended for blacks.

I asked Minor about fried chicken, when it had occurred to him it would be wise to ban it and that he should begin to promote health through his ministry.

"In a Baptist church," he said, "you're not appointed, you're elected. So when I got here I saw these people in all these special sizes. I knew I couldn't just come out and say, 'You got a special size, do something about it.' The same way they elected me, they would have unelected me. So I had to think: what can I do it to get the message across without letting them know it's my message? The summer I became pastor, a minister friend started pastoring another church in the area. We decided to bring back the Rising Sun Usher Federation, a fellowship of church ushers gone dormant. I became director of training. Well, why not make health the biggest part of my training? I didn't tell anybody, since I had an ulterior motive. I started coming back to Oak Hill and telling them that the Rising Sun Usher Federation was pushing health. And it took about five years, but it really started taking hold. We started seeing members shrink, literally shrink. And we ain't got any skinny women or people here now, but you don't have the morbid obese folks like we used to have. People a lot healthier."

Minor is tall and relatively thin; he wears the build of an old athlete. His appearance no doubt helps the persuasion of his platform, but he is no martinet. The embargo on fried foods aside, he is not picky about what he eats and does not spend hours in the gym. Until the Affordable Care Act, he was unable to buy health insurance himself because of a preexisting condition, one that affects his digestive system, and curiously, he is not passionate about health care as such. Rather he says, "I believe in empowering people," and identifies this conviction as a birthright, a fact of his heritage. He can remember his mother telling him it was time to clean out the icebox, after which Minor would walk around to neighboring houses and distribute food he knew was not spoiled. His parents and, later, his grandparents, who adopted him, gave him a comfortable upbringing despite their modest means, and while Minor grew up below the poverty line, he never knew that until his roommates pointed it out to him—at Harvard, which he attended in the 1980s. A scholarship was offered, but Minor wanted to pay for his tuition and held a series of odd jobs, such as serving as a nighttime guard in a housing project in Cambridge.

Unlike many Baptist preachers in the South, Minor did not set out to wear the robe, but when he was almost thirty he had a religious experience: "One Sunday afternoon I was driving back from visiting church. It was bad weather and my car was out of fix. I was going across the bridge and I lost control and it was as if I heard the voice of God saying, 'I got your attention now, I want you to preach for me.'" Still, when talking to him it is the economist who emerges with greater regularity; Minor is one of those who believes the present can be accounted for by pointing to immutable economic law. He once told me you can infer most of what you need to know about a Mississippi town by looking at the number of banks that are open, and which brand of bank at that, and when we describe the various obstacles to reforming the health care system, I start by counting off Tea Party politics and the concerted push of history. But he says only, "There's a lot of money made off poor people and poor health," knowing the drug companies and dialysis clinics all bite off a piece of the insurance companies' largesse.

Minor left Harvard after his junior year to sell cars. He bought expensive clothes and ate hundred-dollar lunches but quit, he says, once he realized there was no way to succeed at such a job without capitalizing on the ignorance of the poor. He returned to Harvard and switched his major from math to economics, and after graduating moved to Memphis and earned master's and doctorate degrees. Every five years, he says, he tries to reinvent himself, and even while pastoring and overseeing the network of navigators he teaches economics for the University of Phoenix and serves as director of outreach for the National Baptist Health Convention.

Ironically, he never intended to get involved with ACA enrollment, believing Mississippi would have the resources to see to it that people were enrolled. "You got to understand," he said, "the ACA was set up for the states to do their own marketplaces." But Washington—Health and Human Services—canceled Mississippi's marketplace, which made Minor realize the importance of the navigator grant. "It dawned on me we have to apply for this," he said, knowing that without some kind of aggressive program, thousands who should sign up and needed to would not.

No other state had its application for a marketplace denied. Mississippi's governor, Phil Bryant, is a Republican and no fan of Obamacare. He opposed the creation of a state marketplace, yet Mississippi's insurance commissioner, Mike Chaney—who is a friend of Bryant's—began setting one up, and even established a web page, onemississippi.org. But Health and Human Services had decreed that each marketplace must offer Medicaid as well as private insurance, and, like most Southern states, Mississippi decided to deny the Medicaid expansion. Health and Human Services maintained that Chaney had no authority over Medicaid, a public program, and Bryant said the exchange lay outside the commissioner's jurisdiction to begin with, and finally Health and Human Services felt they had to deny the state's application altogether. In the final bizarre turn of this small civil war, Governor Bryant thanked the federal government for canceling the state's exchange, though gratitude is not what the statement sounds like: "I have said repeatedly that the health insurance exchanges mandated by Obamacare are not free-market exchanges. Instead, they are a portal to a massive and unaffordable new federal entitlement program. They trigger new taxes on businesses and will ultimately drive more people onto Medicaid rolls. I firmly maintain my position that Mississippi will not willfully implement a mechanism that will compromise our state's financial stability."

That last sentence, "Mississippi will not willfully implement . . ." is a seamless trope, and we have watched it migrate through the generations. The feds must force his hand, in other words, and that sets up the familiar showdown, the Southern governor standing in the schoolhouse door. Bryant alone knows how much his recalcitrance is genuine and how much is grandstanding to please his party. A little more than fifty years ago, one of Bryant's predecessors in Jackson, Ross Barnett, opposed James Meredith's matriculation at Ole Miss. But after it became clear Meredith would be enrolled by federal fiat, Barnett colluded with the Kennedys on how to look best in defeat. He scripted his own martyrdom, made sure he would become the patron saint of segregation, at one point telling the President it would be better all around—better for the show—if the U.S. marshals escorting Meredith pointed their guns at Mississippi militiamen. In the end, Barnett valued white supremacy not so much in itself as for the value it gave his political life.

———

The point of this analogy is not to paint Bryant as a racist, only to say that his outspokenness against Obamacare and Medicaid is determined for him by his voters and donors. The electorate must be pleased, even a frothy electorate, and whatever excites passion, that's where you go; that is the point to be exploited. Sooner or later, though, all that cant and ballyhoo trickle down to the local, human level, and that's where Minor and the navigators come in; they see that level up close, day after day. The realities of Mississippi, to them, are no abstraction, not a political instrument or some means to invoke mythology about states' rights. Mississippi has the highest teen birth rate of any state, the highest number of deaths due to heart disease, and the greatest percentage of obese adults.[*] As of January 2014, some 454,000 residents of the state did not have health insurance.

And because of the refusal to expand Medicaid, there are only so many who can be helped by the Affordable Care Act. An individual must make $11,600 a year to afford any policy offered by the marketplace. And in Mississippi, "you basically have to be almost homeless" to qualify for Medicaid, as Minor put it—or, officially, in the words of the Kaiser Family Foundation: "In Mississippi, Medicaid eligibility for non-disabled adults is limited to parents with incomes below 29% of poverty, or about $6,800 a year for a family of four, and adults without dependent children remain ineligible regardless of their income." Thus, many are not covered in

---

[*] These statistics are courtesy of the Kaiser Family Foundation, as are all others in this chapter, unless otherwise noted.

either direction; they do not make enough to buy health insurance but earn too much somehow to qualify for Medicaid.

"We bring those people in," Minor said, "we don't want to deny them going through the process, but they make too little money. We can't sign them up. A lot of them make less than $11,000 a year. Or they make more but they got a family of four or five. We know we easily could have signed up twice as many people or more, but they just didn't qualify. The Affordable Care Act was not designed for people on $11,000. Nor should it be. We're just offering health insurance. So when the Medicaid expansion was given up to the states to do, it left a place like Mississippi holding the bag. I got nothing for them."

"Every day I come home," Tyler said, "I just get madder with the system. The system is not designed to help the poor. It's designed to help the middle class." She can usually tell as soon as she enters a house whether the people living there make enough money for insurance or not. "I don't want to tell them up front, because I don't want them to think it's me not wanting to do the work, so I put the information in and let the system show. When the system kick it back and the insurance be so high, then you got to tell them about the federally funded place they can go. I got to try to help them some kind of way; I don't want to just leave them out there in the cold."

There are nearly 300,000 individuals in Mississippi who are ineligible for either option, insurance or Medicaid, and as Tyler said, the most she can do is refer them to a federally qualified community health center, an imperfect solution since transportation, as noted, is not widely available in the Delta.* Minor has been calling churches and asking ministers to use their buses and vans to bring people to the health center and back; after all, he told me,

---

* The figure of close to 300,000 comes from Reuters: "Mississippi Blues: The cost of rejecting Medicaid expansion" by Julie Steenhuysen, www.reuters.com, October 4, 2013.

those vehicles sit mostly unused in the parking lot all week. I asked about house calls. He said that was a good idea in theory, though the physician was liable to get jumped when entering a home, and their drugs stolen. Someone from the ministry, he said, would have to go along with the doctor.

I felt stupid, in any case, to be talking about house calls in the year 2014, reviewing old methods, old solutions. So I steered our conversation to the subject with which our introduction began. "Do you believe health care is a civil right?" I asked.

"I believe it is a human right."

"And by that you mean it is a right we are all born with?"

"Yes. Eventually everybody ought to be in a position where they can pay for it, but until you get to that position . . . if I'm a child, then I should be on my parents' plan at no charge. At some point I get a job and pay for it myself. Economics was my major. I hate the free-rider thing. If you make things totally free, people overuse it."

For me these answers nullify one another, for anything that is a human right should be kept out of commerce, a realm just as apt to be abused as any in which things are given without cost. But as we continue talking, it comes out there is another reason Minor does not believe health care will be nationalized in America. "Our population is so heterogeneous," he says, meaning that if "you don't look like me, you don't have the same concern. Shouldn't be that way, but it is." For him people naturally reserve their highest sympathies for those of a similar appearance and background. At the same time he is optimistic about the future and speaks often of what he calls the "hip-hop generation" and how they are able to look beyond race. "It's going to change. I may not see it, but I know it will. This new hip-hop generation sees people as people. I'm confident that we will see a day when race won't be an issue in Mississippi."

"History says the opposite," I told him. "History says race is tenacious."

But he was unmoved: "The internet, Twitter, all this stuff, the influx of Hispanics. They're neither white nor black—they bridge the gap."

He continued citing reasons, like the fact that church attendance is down among young whites, meaning fewer will be exposed to the racist pronouncements, thinly disguised, of the Southern Baptist denomination. And other structures that enforce racism, he said, are not as prevalent as they were in his boyhood.

My response was to ask, "Would you agree you're an optimistic person by temperament?" It was my way of dismissing his vision of an America without prejudice or considerations of race, of indicating the idea was ridiculous to me. He realized my intention and said, "Look, I never thought I'd see the day a black church would get a federal grant to do outreach in Mississippi. That's making progress, big time."

"But the lesson of the Obama presidency is that we're still a deeply racist nation."

We went around and around until there was nothing to do except note that it was both ironic and a sign of progress that in this colloquy it was the older Southern black man, the great-grandson of a slave, saying no, race will one day cease to be a factor in American life, while the younger white man was making the opposite case, for racism's perennial force and perennial evil.

But ironies and reversals aside, the question remains: is health care a civil right? Really, when someone asks this question they are giving voice to another, more generalized query: is this a legal movement or a quality-of-life movement? There is no mention of health care in the Constitution or the Bill of Rights. As a result the Supreme Court has never had to rule definitively on the question. Desegregation and the franchise came to the movement heavily armed. One could always invoke the language of the 14th and 15th Amendments when mounting a challenge. But health care, while notionally, I suppose, part of the pursuit of happiness—

not something we want to anatomize or legislate—has no similar foundation, no clear legal precedent or appeal.

Still, the conditions are the same on many fronts, even if the legal framework is not. As with the vote or education, you find a lack of access and quality shifting along racial lines. And the history reads the same. Jim Crow was once as permanent a feature of hospitals as it was of restaurants or hotels. In the early 1960s, it is pointed out with great frequency, few African Americans in Mississippi and other Deep South states had ever voted in an election. Well, few had ever seen a doctor, either. In the Delta if you had a job it was likely on a plantation, and there were no sick days; if you fell ill you slogged through it and waited, or hoped, to get better. And if you were unemployed, as many were, once cotton picking was turned over to machines, there was no way of seeking care. "In such an environment," wrote historian John Dittmer in his book *The Good Doctors*, "where one had to choose between food, rent, and medicine, good health was almost impossible."

As the civil rights movement gained momentum in those years, it focused on other priorities. Recently I read through the major speeches given at the March on Washington in 1963. There is not a sustained mention of health care in any of them, and when you turn to the ten-point petition that was circulated at the march —"What We Demand" is the paper's heading—you come across mention of housing, jobs, the vote, and education, but nothing about doctors or clinics. The same can be said for an anthology titled *Freedom Now!*, published in 1964, with contributors such as James Baldwin and Malcolm X. It contains sections devoted to "Discrimination in Public Accommodations," "Denial of Housing to Negroes," and "Discrimination Against Negroes in Law Enforcement," but there is not a single chapter or essay on health care. Perform other tests, and they yield similar results. If these years are to be described as the movement's prime—"the classical period" in Rustin's phrase—then the issue doesn't appear to have made serious claims on the attention of the leadership.*

But if the leadership seldom spoke of health care in those days, there were others who did. A contingent of two hundred, called the Medical Committee for Civil Rights, was present at the March on Washington in 1963. In the past, they had picketed the segregated practices of the American Medical Association. A year later, a cadre of doctors and nurses who had decided to provide treatment to Freedom Summer staff and volunteers founded the Medical Committee for Human Rights. The Delta Ministry, a coalition sponsored by the National Council of Churches, was also formed in Mississippi in 1964 and made health care one focus of its organizing. These groups all cooperated, and their legacy is everywhere today. "The comprehensive community health center movement," wrote Dittmer, "was the most significant and enduring achievement in the field of health care to come out of the civil rights years. Discussions held by Jack Geiger, Count Gibson, Bob Smith, and other MCHR activists in Mississippi in the fall of 1964 led to the Office of Economic Opportunity's funding of two centers, one in the Columbia Point section of Boston and the other in a rural southern community."

The site chosen for the rural South was Mound Bayou in the Delta's Bolivar County. The Tufts-Delta Health Center opened in 1967 with a staff of nine: three doctors, five nurses and one social worker. They provided care for no charge; more than eight thousand patients visited the clinic during its first two years of operation. Many suffered from starvation, and sometimes prescriptions

---

* There is the famous remark ascribed to King, "of all the forms of inequality, injustice in health care is the most shocking and inhumane," but the lineage of the quote is difficult to trace, and we will never know for sure if he made the statement or not. It was allegedly delivered at a conference in Chicago in 1966, but no text or recording of the speech exists. The aphorism may well have evolved over time, attributable to hearsay, becoming one of those catchalls that people in need of an imprimatur cite.

were written for nothing but food. Meanwhile, a greater lobby was mobilizing around the issue, and in the spring of 1968 the Poor People's Campaign was launched. Martin Luther King had been shot in April, and Bayard Rustin was named coordinator of the Solidarity Day March, a major rally staged in June of that year. When he drafted a list of demands to accompany the demonstration, health care was out in front—as one might expect, given the correlations between health and income. "Is there a meaningful right to life," he asked, "when the Department of Agriculture tells us that nearly 20 million Americans are deprived of necessary nutrition because they are poor?" Rustin also made requests of the president, calling for an executive mandate that would create better health services in rural zones and "organize maternal and child health centers in poverty areas."

One can see, in other words, the issue becoming more central as the sixties wore on. But the story remains unfinished. Momentum never crested on this score as it did in other areas; the reasons for that are several, but one is that the supporting institutions or networks vanished. The Poor People's Campaign was short-lived; the Delta Ministry folded in the 1970s, and the Medical Committee for Human Rights in the 1980s. If the best substitute for legal precedent is historical precedent, the issue waits again to be pulled in from the periphery. There are signs that this is already taking place. Early in 2014, the Moral Monday movement spread into Georgia. In March, thirty-nine people were arrested at the statehouse in Atlanta after protesting the rejection of the Medicaid expansion. Some shouted and held up banners as the Senate began conducting business. Others sat down outside the governor's office, blocking the door, waiting to be arrested. It was a diverse group, as Moral Monday was in North Carolina, comprised of college students and farmers and even the pastor of Ebenezer Baptist Church, where King and his father preached.

Later that year Bob Zellner marched to Washington, D.C.,

with the mayor of Belhaven, North Carolina, to protest the closing of a clinic in that town. Funding for Vidant Pungo Hospital ran out when the state opted not to expand Medicaid. For some in the area it is now a trip greater than eighty miles to the nearest hospital, and a week after the clinic closed a forty-eight-year-old woman died while waiting for a medevac. "If the governor and legislature don't want to accept Medicaid expansion," said Adam O'Neal, the Belhaven mayor and a staunch Republican, "they need to come up with another program to assure that rural hospitals don't close. They're allowing people to die to prove a point." He paced the march, in excess of two hundred miles, over fifteen days, and when he reached the Capitol a rally was held. Joining O'Neal was Crystal Price, an employee of Wendy's. She is twenty-seven years old; she has cervical cancer and no health insurance. "They don't want to expand Medicaid, so families like mine," she said, "have to decide whether they're going to pay for our children's health care or our own."

And that's it, I said to myself when reading the story in the *Washington Post*. You won't find a better definition of the problem of health care. Some people, as Dittmer suggested, have to make tough choices. Others don't. And in the triage of poverty—can I take five hours away from work, and risk getting fired, to visit the clinic?—health is going to win out once the situation has become critical, but usually not before. Make care more affordable, more available, through insurance or Medicaid, and the pressure of choice is reduced; seeing to that, it seems to me, should be a priority of the civil rights movement. Of course, bringing health care into the movement also means bringing the inevitable tensions into it as well. When I told Minor about the demonstration in Georgia, he was unimpressed.

"It's good for the symbolism," he said, "but it's not the answer." When I asked what is the answer, he said they had to get the hospitals involved, petition the states, move behind the scenes—

"make them see. The more we talk about it, the more we can get the word out, start creating a mass of people, at some point you'll reach a tipping point."

It was perhaps the oldest tenet of organizing; Minor believed the best way to proceed was not through some dilemma action, a march or a sit-in, but instead to make a concerted push at the grassroots.

"And get more people involved who don't look like me—that helps." Here was the part of his strategy that pointed to the role of race in particular. In Minor's view, the only way Mississippi would ever become amenable to the Affordable Care Act was if the hospital executives and legislators were made to understand that the marketplace helped a wide swath of the citizenry, not just poor African Americans. As he had told me at our initial meeting, most of those he had helped guide through the enrollment process were white.

"I think there are places in the nation," Minor said about opposition to Obamacare, "where it is a philosophical thing about government, but down here, it's a hundred percent race politics. Get the government out, farming would collapse down here. That's why you don't hear that argument about big government; farm subsidies make this thing work. There's a stereotype of who these people are. So we're trying to say, look, it's not who they think it is—"

And here I couldn't help but wonder, so what if they are? That was the implication of Minor's comment: if you are poor and black then you are unworthy of attention, so we cannot rest our case with you; we must go out and make some broader appeal. Are there supposed to be untouchables in a democracy?

—"and really break down the numbers of who these people are and where they are. In Mississippi there are more poor white people than black people. Also get the hospitals involved, to show how they would be better served because of no free care. We're ultimately paying for it, the people who do have insurance, because they have to jack up the price to cover those who can't pay."

A logical assault, in other words, except it would amount to lobbying a constituency that doesn't always think logically. "Well who benefits from not providing health care to the poor?" I asked. "Aside from the ideologues, who benefits?"

"Nobody benefits," Minor answered.

"It's the opposite, right? You just said it: those who do have insurance, your typical citizen who gets it through their employer, they're the ones who bear the brunt. It doesn't make sense."

"Remember we were talking about my hometown? And I told you the black school is still standing, and the white school tore down? It makes no sense either. Things happen in the South, people do because of ideology or whatever, make no sense—but they do it anyhow. I lived through it. It makes no sense but it happens."

It makes no sense but it happens. There does seem to be an element of illogic, or even of suicide or martyrdom, attached to the South. The region acts as its own worst enemy and moves constantly against its interests, for it is the South, ultimately, that chooses to come in last in all the education and health statistics. Refusing to care for its poor seemed part of the same complex.

But Minor also conveyed an important virtue of the Southerner; life in Mississippi, he seemed to say, bred an acceptance of the uncanny, and I saw that on some level it was fruitless to try to reason your way out of the labyrinth of American reality, as I had attempted that night I left John Perdew and drove to Alabama. The experiences of Minor's life had given him a different turn of mind, one that was largely free of the impulse to unlock everything, to create a precise and orderly arrangement. He had made his peace with lived contradiction—and long ago, I suspected.

———

As we drove through Coldwater, Minor pointed out a patch of dirt, the surface smooth, gleaming, and uniform: a building site. "That's my pride and joy," he said. Till recently, the lot had belonged to a funeral home, but it had burned to the ground. Minor bought the land and secured funding for a community health center. It had taken him five years. Originally he wanted to build in Hernando, but Hernando is full of people who work in Memphis, people with money, and any health center established there would not be eligible for federal qualification. So Minor turned his attention to Coldwater, his hometown.

"It opened this month," he said in August 2014, "and has really been a godsend, not only an opportunity for people to get quality health care, but also create jobs, receptionists and janitorial staff. Matter of fact, they're going to name the clinic after him"—he was referring to the mortician, the old owner. "It's going to be a running joke. Used to be, if you going to M.J. Edwards you going to see a dead body; now you going to M.J. Edwards you going to a clinic. The irony of a place that was putting folks in the ground, at the end of life, now it's into life."

Like Septima Clark and Bernice Robinson, Minor and Tyler serve as reminders that the gamesmanship of the state, the rhetoric pumped out of catered policy dinners in air-conditioned boardrooms, can always be countered by an everyday determination and feelings of neighborly regard. "We try to cover every county," Tyler said, and recalled a diabetic she helped to buy insurance. It was a classic tale of healing, the marks of sickness being slowly wiped away: "I said, you make sure you get in there and get that preventative health care. She be going to the doctor now, and used to have dark circles, spots, but they're gone from under her eyes. It's amazing, a blessing. And imagine if all the people who couldn't get it could get it."

It may not seem like a fair fight. It's a two-front war, as she is up against the Delta and its fixity, its obdurate patterns of living, as well as the Jackson power elite. Tyler doesn't sleep much during enrollment periods. Her shift at Parchman ends at eight in the morning, and she is home for only a moment, to gather her hotspot and tablet before setting out into the country. If someone can't enroll in either Medicaid or the marketplace, she drives them to the community health center or writes down phone numbers of those who can, or just sits awhile, trying to lift spirits. "I got to give them something" is her motto. And on reflection, there's no cause to ask if it's a fair fight or not. Because women like that, they're never overmatched.

My days in Mississippi put me in touch with the grand design of organizing. No matter where it took place, I saw, be it the Low Country of South Carolina or across the fields and hamlets of the Delta, it meant figuring out how pliable the existing arrangement of things was, and then attempting to find the room for maneuver. History will not always glorify or record this sort of work, and Minor even said he preferred it that way, to carry on invisibly and move behind the scenes, yet I knew that his modesty on this score did not translate to a smallness of ambition. Because he hoped to create a larger consensus over the next couple of years, he had said, to raise awareness of the issue beyond the Delta, beyond Mississippi, and in so doing reach a tipping point.

When he told me of this plan I thought: Well, I know two men who did just that, fifty years ago. They had organized in small towns and met strenuous opposition from the state, but persisted until the nation as a whole took notice. The emphasis in those days was on the vote, and now Robert Moses and David Dennis work in the schools, to improve the education of America's poor, black, and Latino students. And in this setting the lessons of the past can help only so much. For it was tougher, they said; as hard as it was for me to believe—and for a long time I could not believe it—each maintained that this current phase of the struggle was acted out against longer odds, an even greater resistance, than the campaign for the vote had been all those decades ago.

2.

Robert Moses and David Dennis arrived in Mississippi in 1961. The state was becoming known in movement circles as a place unto itself. It may not look different, crossing over from Alabama or Louisiana, yet as John Lewis put it to me: "You get to Mississippi, your disposition changes completely, because you're on your way to a different world. You felt that."

Dennis was a student at Dillard University in New Orleans. He had recently joined the campus chapter of CORE, the Congress of Racial Equality, the group responsible for the Freedom Rides, sending black and white passengers on a bus journey across the South in May 1961. They were testing enforcement of a federal law forbidding segregation in the ticket offices and restaurants of bus depots. In Anniston, Alabama, one of the buses carrying the riders was bombed and the other set on by a mob. The Freedom Riders were beaten, and a few of them, after receiving cursory medical care in Alabama, were brought to New Orleans for treatment. Dennis's CORE affiliates felt strongly that the rides should continue, that it must not appear as though they could be stopped by intimidation or reprisal. They decided to travel to Montgomery, purchase their own bus tickets, and resume the trek west, through Mississippi and back to New Orleans. Dennis did not want to go, but his friends bought him a round of cocktails, and when he got on the train to Montgomery he was slightly drunk. Students from Nashville—Diane Nash and others—also went

to Alabama to provide reinforcement, and by this time the Freedom Rides had captured the attention of all of America, the White
House included.

"The most difficult thing," Dennis said, "was getting to the
bus station. We had to go through a mob of people. The bus was
also boarded by National Guard, because the city was under mar-
tial law; also the Kennedys had decided they were going to provide this protection. The bus went nonstop to the Mississippi line,
and there the National Guard from Mississippi boarded that bus;
we didn't even stop for people to go to the restroom. We traveled
straight through, National Guard in front and back of the bus, and
also helicopters going over, and you had segregationists lining the
highway, screaming and yelling as we drove down the road.

"Then when we got to Jackson, there was a line of police officers on each side of the door of the bus, and the line sort of formed
a corridor right into the white waiting room, which we walked
into from the bus. If you wanted to go in another direction you
couldn't, because the police had formed this corridor. Once we
got inside, the chief of police told us we were not allowed to be on
that side; we were violating the law of the state of Mississippi and
we were all under arrest. We then were marched straight out of
another door and into a paddy wagon."

Dennis, along with many other Freedom Riders, was sent to
Parchman. The prisoners endured a variety of taunts and torture
and threats, but for Dennis, as for John Perdew, the days in jail
helped to confirm his resolve. When he returned to New Orleans he
became more active in CORE and began leading demonstrations.

The controversy stirred by the Freedom Rides, meanwhile,
disrupted Robert Moses's plan. He had moved to Mississippi that
summer, opting not to renew his teaching contract at Horace
Mann, an elite preparatory academy in the Bronx. He thought he
would be starting a voter registration campaign in the little Delta town of Cleveland. But Amzie Moore, Moses's mentor, a gas

station owner who had connections to the NAACP and who had attempted registration drives of his own, advised him it would be wise to start somewhere else, as the Freedom Rides had set everyone on edge. Moses ended up in the southwestern part of the state. C.C. Bryant, a Freemason and president of the local NAACP, offered to host registration classes in a Masonic Temple in McComb. It was SNCC's first project in Mississippi, and initially an operation of one, as Moses worked by himself. The task was Herculean. McComb is the seat of Pike County, where eight-thousand African Americans lived, though only two hundred were registered—plenty, compared to the counties on either side. In Amite to the west, one black was listed as being eligible to vote, and none in Walthall to the east.

Moses was twenty-five, older than everyone else in SNCC. In high school he had won a scholarship to Hamilton College in upstate New York, where the student body contained only two other African Americans. After earning a degree in philosophy, he enrolled in Harvard and had finished his master's when he was called home to Harlem. His mother died in 1958 and while mourning his father had suffered a nervous collapse. Moses moved back to New York and took a job as a math teacher at Horace Mann. Soon thereafter an inner frustration he was fitfully in touch with found a wider expression: "The sit-ins hit me powerfully," he has said, "in the soul as well as the brain. I was mesmerized by the pictures I saw almost every day on the front pages of the *New York Times*—young committed Black faces seated at lunch counters or picketing, directly and with great dignity, challenging white supremacy in the South. They looked like I felt."

Moses spent the summer of 1960 in Atlanta, working in the offices of the Southern Christian Leadership Conference. The assignment was full of lonely office work, not quite what he had envisioned, and he volunteered to go on a recruiting trip for SNCC. He visited the states of the Deep South for the first time. Amzie

Moore, he saw, was advocating a different tack than most. "He wasn't distracted by school integration," Moses recalled. "He was for it, but it didn't distract him from the centrality of the right to vote. He wasn't distracted about the integration of public facilities. It was a good thing, but it was not going straight to the heart of what was the trouble in Mississippi. Somehow, in following his guidance there, we stumbled on the key—the right to vote and the political action that ensued."

Nothing about voter registration was easy. The locals in Pike, Amite, and Walthall were tentative, and those who did volunteer to visit the courthouse could expect to be harassed. Moses did have the ear of a few in the Justice Department—the 1957 Civil Rights Act had contained provisions about interfering with registration—but federal oversight or protection was limited. Seeking help, Moses visited New Orleans, and that's when he met Dennis, who not long after became CORE's Mississippi director. In 1962 an alliance was formed, the Council of Federated Organizations, "better known as COFO," as Dennis said, "which Bob Moses and myself were co-directors of. We sort of merged everybody into it. SNCC workers were COFO workers; CORE workers were COFO workers. We felt we would do that to keep from having any real competition among the organizations. On the national level that would hurt what we were doing in Mississippi."

They pressed on under this new aegis, doing what they could. The nation's attention seized on Mississippi now and then, particularly after the murder of Medgar Evers, but few African Americans were added to the voter rolls, and all the while the violence carried on. Both men, by rights, should have died in Mississippi, and both built up, in their various ways, elemental defenses, became reconciled to the presence of death in their daily routines. "We lived every day as if it was our last," Dennis said. In February 1963 Moses was riding in a Buick that was shot up. The windows blew out and the driver slumped against him. Moses somehow was able to catch his weight and find the brake. They were seven miles outside Greenwood, in an empty stretch of the Delta, and would have no means of escape if the assailants chose to turn around and finish the job. But they did not.

One reason for the Mississippi Summer Project was that America did not seem to care about all the violence that was being waged in Mississippi. "You didn't get a lot of attention, a lot of outrage from this country," Dennis said. "And we felt the reason why is that people losing their lives in the danger zone were not the country's children."

If that was the central, animating question of Freedom Summer—whom do we look upon as being the country's children?—it is also one, we shall see, that has haunted Moses and Dennis throughout their second acts in the movement. That was the aim of Freedom Summer, to round up the children of this country; and they were young and white and from the North and generally affluent. If something happened to them, people noticed, as Howard Kirschenbaum realized when he was arrested that night in Moss Point. "When we got out," he said, "there were two lawyers from Jackson who had come down overnight. We had been seen being arrested, fortunately. And I was told to place two phone calls. One was to Senator Kenneth Keating from New York. And I called his office and they said, 'I just want to say we're looking out for you and we admire what you're doing,' and I thought to myself: Boy, this is just what they organized the Mississippi Summer Project for. How many blacks had gone to jail in Mississippi and been beaten and worse without anybody paying attention, and after this relatively mild incident on my part a U.S. Senator is making a phone call for my protection."

Almost a thousand volunteers would travel to Mississippi between June and August of 1964. They were put in harm's way, a decision that placed the civil rights movement in new territory, Machiavellian territory, you might say. For the first time, there was talk of ends justifying means, whereas in Greensboro or Birmingham that phrase had seldom been heard. The philosophy of nonviolent witness is easy to understand: it actualizes, if only on a small scale, the vision of the protestor. Sitting-in takes a segregated diner, a corrupt space, and in one stroke turns it into an open and democratized community. Morally, the act is unimpeachable. But with the Mississippi Summer Project the vocabulary changes. Now the movement had to consider the value of "necessary sacrifices," or whether an evil and ruthless system demands a response that is itself calculating. And it would not play out in diners or city streets before countless onlookers, but in the woods and along the back roads of Mississippi, in the absolute darkness that befell the state at night.

The volunteers were briefed on the danger, which raises yet another question—and the Summer Project is like that; it can seem at times an ethical hall of mirrors. Are you still a sacrifice if you assent to your own doom? At the orientation held in Oxford, Ohio, Moses encouraged many to go home, and the tragic prophecy was fulfilled on day one, a Sunday. On June 21, 1964, James Chaney, Michael Schwerner, and Andrew Goodman were arrested for speeding in Philadelphia, Mississippi. They spent the day in jail and were executed upon their release that night. Dennis was close to both Schwerner and Chaney; those two had been working for CORE in Meridian, Mississippi, since January of that year. They drove to Philadelphia on June 21 to investigate the remains of a church that had been firebombed earlier in the week. Dennis had contemplated going with them, but decided he was too sick, as he had come down that week with bronchitis. He went home to Shreveport, instead. I asked him once how often he thinks about June 21, and his answer was simple and direct. "I don't ever stop," he said.

And that was when I began to understand the vast dimensions of all that was given up or traded in those years. History tells us much about the physical penalty, the murders and beatings, but the mind does as much or more suffering. "In June or July 1964," Dennis also told me, "I walked out of the COFO office. It was late at night. A car drove up and this guy pulled a shotgun out and said, 'Ready to die, nigger?' And I just started laughing; I couldn't stop laughing. It threw them off for a minute, then somebody came out of the office, started screaming, and they drove off. And I'm sitting there, still laughing."

Scores of theories have been proposed to explain why the movement lost momentum after Selma. It was Watts,* they say, or a loss of faith in nonviolence, Vietnam pushing everyone's attention elsewhere, and King's death, and so on. But what if the answer is more basic and attritional—if it simply came down to a generation being divested of its energy? Events of the late sixties no doubt had their effect—but "complicating all this," said Charlie Cobb, another field secretary for SNCC, "was the simple fact that we were tired." And Dennis: "We didn't know anything about this post-trauma stuff at that time. Now they say living under those conditions, you shouldn't do for more than six months. We did it for three, five years. All of us had to have some damage."

Freedom Summer, indeed, was the end of the line for Dennis and Moses—or at least it seemed that way at the time. A year later Dennis was in law school at the University of Michigan. After earning his J.D., he established a practice in New Orleans. Over the next couple of decades, many he had known in the movement took to the speaking circuit, visiting college campuses and giving motivational talks, but Dennis stayed quiet. He granted few interviews and authored no books.

---

* The neighborhood of Los Angeles where rioting occurred in August of 1965, less than a week after Lyndon Johnson signed the Voting Rights Act into law. The riot was seen as a sign that the peaceful tactics favored by some leaders of the movement were limited in their effect and appeal, and the loss of property and life in Los Angeles shifted the opinion of many whites who had previously held sympathy for the African American struggle.

Moses's crack-up, if you want to call it that, was a public affair. In February 1965, SNCC gathered in Atlanta to air grievances and debate a possible restructuring. Moses announced that henceforth he was adopting the maiden name of his mother, and gave a wandering monologue, part memoir and part philosophy, that wound up: "From now on I am Bob Parris, and I will no longer speak to white people." He distanced himself from SNCC. In the ensuing months, some spotted him around the South, alone in a field, sipping whiskey, and he began to protest the escalation of military activity in Vietnam. The following year he was drafted, though he was thirty-one and past the legal age of induction. Moses believed he was being punished for speaking out against the war; he went to Canada and later to Tanzania, teaching math in a village school for the next ten years while raising a family with his second wife, Janet.

He returned to the United States after President Carter pardoned those who had evaded their draft summons, and became a student again at Harvard. He assumed his old name and began talking to historians. In 1982, his daughter Maisha entered eighth grade at Martin Luther King Middle School in Cambridge, Massachusetts. The school did not offer basic algebra. With the permission of Maisha's teacher, Moses began visiting the class, tutoring her and three others. "I saw three distinct groupings," he said of Maisha's class, "mostly upper-middle-class white kids above grade level; a better racial mix of kids at grade level, mostly middle-class; and kids below grade level who were primarily minority students and working-class whites. This skewing of math along racial and class lines had the effect of sending the message to students of color that little was expected of them. So I began thinking about who takes math, and what kind of math they take." The next year Maisha and the others who had studied with Moses passed Boston's standardized test for algebra. They were the first members of their school ever to do so.

A nonprofit was created. Moses also received one of the "genius grants" awarded by the MacArthur Foundation. He left Harvard. From the beginning he insisted the Algebra Project had more to do with civil rights than education reform. Many, including his old COFO partner, were unable to see the connection. "Poor Bob," Dennis admitted to thinking when learning about the Algebra Project. "He's lost his mind."

The two had not seen each other since Freedom Summer when a reunion was held in Jackson in the spring of 1988. The Chaney, Goodman, and Schwerner murders had recently become the subject of a film, *Mississippi Burning*, which glamorized the FBI, telling of two agents who work tirelessly to identify and convict the conspirators. A lot of license was invoked to fashion this plot; the FBI, it's true, through Klan informants and thousands of dollars in bribes, was able to locate the bodies and establish a reliable chronology of what occurred on June 21. But J. Edgar Hoover was no ally of the movement. He regarded the Summer Project as a communist enterprise, and *Mississippi Burning* upset many movement alums. A curious thing had happened to them: they had become history, and they convened in Jackson to vent frustration over the movie but also to address a larger question. Lots of movies and books would be made about their lives and the times they helped to shape. Could they exert any control over these portrayals? What might they do to make them more accurate?

During the reunion, Moses and Dennis stayed in Jackson's Edison Wathall Hotel. In the early mornings they sat by the pool and relived old times. Moses described his vision for the Algebra Project, why he believed it to be the next frontier of the struggle for civil rights. Dennis was skeptical, but when Moses asked for his help, he said he would give it. He visited schools in Chicago that were using the Algebra Project's methods and saw the morass of unlearning, the frightened teachers and subpar facilities, the league of students who had developed a habit or front of indifference.

Soon Dennis had given up lawyering, moved to Jackson, and taken over the Southern Initiative of the Algebra Project. Returning to Mississippi after more than a quarter century, he said, was like getting religion. "When I left Mississippi, I felt that there was a part of me missing. I didn't finish something."

The friendship between Moses and Dennis may amount to the longest ongoing collaboration in the movement, but it must strike some as unlikely, since the personality of one is the antipode of the other. Dennis is from the South, Moses from the North. Dennis is portly, loves Cajun food and Crown Royal, and can name every barbecue shack in Mississippi or Alabama. Some, like Dreamland in Tuscaloosa and Big Daddy's in Meridian, he has been patronizing for more than half a century. Moses is a vegetarian, swam laps at dawn for many years, and has a measured, studious demeanor. Dennis is fidgety and outgoing, and though he looks fierce in the most widely circulated footage of him—showing the emotional eulogy he delivered for James Chaney—he is quite funny, pushing humor into spaces one would never expect. I've heard him relate a story about a church bombing and have everyone doubled over in laughter.

And there are more fundamental differences. The two do not have the same beliefs about strategy, Moses told me once. He believes it important for the young in a community to maintain their autonomy, hold to their own sect; Dennis wants everyone to sit at the same table, so to speak, and share an equal voice. Mississippi and the decades of partnership is what the two men have in common, and that is more than enough. They're like brothers, Dennis has said, though as is true of many siblings, they can only be in the same room for so long before familiar disputes are revisited.

When meeting Moses, as with John Lewis, you notice the voice first. It has not changed much since Freedom Summer; it's soft and reflective, and he speaks slowly enough that you don't need a recorder when interviewing him, for you have time enough to transcribe. His features are not as delicate as what you see in documentaries and old newsreels; over the years the sockets have deepened, or just appear to have, now that he no longer wears glasses. The hair has been wiped away and the jaw become squarer and so more prominent. He is abstemious, refusing not only meat and eggs but also liquor and coffee, and there is an air of melancholy or inwardness, which can be spotted easily since Moses is incapable of affectation. He does not assume a separate persona when going out in public. During panel talks he will sit hunched with his eyes closed, and it looks like he has fallen asleep though it will soon become clear he was listening the whole time. The overall effect is less one of eccentricity than of deliberation—extreme mental deliberation.

It is easy to understand what made Dennis a successful organizer. One loves to be around him, not an insignificant quality to have when calling a mass meeting. Moses had to earn the trust of Mississippians in other ways, with his commitment, his tirelessness; it was not unheard-of for him to sustain a beating on his way to the courthouse and keep marching anyway, walking up to the registrar's desk with blood streaming down his face. That was someone sharecroppers would listen to, even if he was from New York and asking them to risk their lives.

Today, people listen to Robert Moses in no small part because he is Robert Moses. He is always going to be the keynote, the main attraction in any room that he enters. Moses has never been comfortable with the attention that accrues to him, and discusses his life in a very selective sense. It's not that he is shying away from unseemly facts; he simply sees the celebrity game as lying outside of, and maybe in opposition to, the main business of the movement. For many, though, his silence and enigmatic ways have only contributed to his mythological status. One Freedom Summer volunteer, in a letter home, described him this way: "He is more or less the Jesus of the whole Project, not because he asks to be, but because of everyone's reaction to him." For fifty years now, Moses has been bound to this paradox, preferring to be invisible yet constantly mediated by lofty and messianic language.

His humility, however, does have practical effects, and humility, you might even say, is his chosen method. I thought about that one day while watching him engage with half a dozen college students. We were seated at a circular table in a meeting room at the College of Charleston. The students were nervous, having read all week about McComb and Freedom Summer, and a few were dressed in bow ties and suspenders. Moses collected their names, asked a question, and then withdrew, declining to say anything further. It was slow going at first, but eventually the participants relaxed and the conversation assumed a life of its own. When Moses did interject, it was in a purely reflexive way, to make students more aware of the language they were using and its implications. He asked one to repeat a question he had stated and then had everyone else paraphrase it, so we might hear the ways in which the question had been understood differently.

Organizing, it occurred to me, must feel a lot like teaching most of the time. Or at least like one kind of teaching, where you strive to create a framework that allows and even demands your own absence, reentering as needed, to focus the discussion. That way, the creativity derives from the collective, not the leader or figurehead. And then I remembered that Moses is a teacher, though not usually thought of that way. But he taught before SNCC and after, and is still teaching today; in fact, when you do the reckoning you realize his days canvassing in Mississippi do not even add up to one-tenth of his life.

His first teaching job was at Horace Mann, one of the best private schools in New York and, ironically, one that more than a few Freedom Summer volunteers attended. Mississippi, with its shack towns and system of peonage, was a revelation. "There was nothing," he told me, "that prepared me for the level of education we encountered in in the Delta. On the one hand, under separate education black schools produced really educated black people. There are prime examples of that. But on the other it also was a dumbing down, the idea that you really are going to give people the minimum. Some of the volunteers coming from Northern colleges stayed and taught at Tougaloo—the level of the students at Tougaloo, it was early high school. So we saw all that."

And that was when I asked if he had been formulating ideas all along, even unconsciously, about what might be done to correct the yawning problem of minority education. He said no, he could not envision an answer back then. That answer, of course, would come two decades later, when Maisha started eighth grade. The Algebra Project's immediate focus is on students and their relationship to math—what goes on in the classroom. Typically the discipline enters the mind as a juggle of laws and procedures. Its existence for most of us is strictly hypothetical: when presented with this, do that. The manipulation of one formula after another is how the discipline gets taught. But to parse a scroll of letters and digits and come out with a number represents the performance of math, not the learning of it, and in crafting his curriculum Moses hoped to avoid the former as much as possible. "In the Algebra Project," he said, "we are using a version of experiential learning; it starts with where the children are, experiences that they share. We get them to reflect on these drawing on their common culture, then to form abstract conceptualizations out of their reflection, and then to apply the abstraction back on their experience."

I spent several days with the Southern Initiative of the Algebra Project in Petersburg, Virginia. One morning I was in a class that was asked a question but told not to invoke a formula when solving it. Instead we were supposed to reason the problem, attempt to tackle it imaginatively. The problem was this: it takes me thirty minutes to walk to school, my brother forty. If he leaves six minutes before I do, when will I overtake him? One woman drew two rows of squares on the blackboard. Four was written inside the ones on top, three in those below. Another used the chessboard floor design and simulated the walk, with each tile representing one minute. A few of us—the true dunces and math wannabes—flailed around unsystematically for a while. I felt confident going with the sixteenth minute, for if the faster of the two reaches the halfway point in fifteen minutes, she or he is one minute behind the brother, who takes twenty to get there but has that head start of six. The correct answer, of course, is eighteen. A normal math class would utilitze the midpoint formula, and that would be that, the work of ten seconds. You thus know what to do when confronted with the problem on a test, but you do not understand. To understand you must cloak the principle in some real life variant.

The Algebra Project's pedagogy may sound unorthodox, but it reminds you that education can do more than provide the path to a job and income. One thinks of James Baldwin's essay "Stranger in the Village," in which he says, "The root function of language is to control the universe by describing it." The lessons Moses devised have the potential of conferring that descriptive power, for mathematical visualization, like the *logos*, can be a way of mapping the world, and whatever is mapped can be defined, assayed, overcome. Teachers who have been trained by the Project will often ask their students to write about the meaning of a problem or of the relationship between quantities as though they were characters in a story. The philosophy runs: if you are constantly being asked to represent what you learn while you are learning it, math will become more than a game or something to be dutifully endured.

"That was when I really began to take ownership of the way I was learning," said Albert Sykes, who is thirty-one today and learned algebra from Moses at Brinkley Middle School in Jackson. The structure of those classes, as Sykes described them, reminded me of the discussion I had witnessed at the College of Charleston.

The goal, he said, was for him to start "thinking of myself as more than a learner but also as a person who was learning to be able to teach. I'd say it was the most freeing education experience I ever had in my life. Teachers didn't let us communicate. You were discouraged from helping each other and talking to each other; then you got Bob telling us you have responsibility to make sure everybody in the room is learning what they need to learn, to get you from this class to the next class."

O'Shai Robinson, who served as president of the Baltimore Algebra Project during his final year of college, stressed the need to root math in familiar settings, to break down its technical language and reinvent it, however you can. He uses games when tutoring—Twister as a means of teaching probability—and asks students to draw pictures, all in the hopes, he said, of locating "a common experience, and not talking about it as math. The concepts are not difficult. The way they are presented is where they get stuck." I told him I had spoken once with a teacher who had contested a standardized test problem. The question revolved around computing the gratuity for a waiter or waitress, and most of her students, the teacher said, had never been out to eat at a restaurant. Robinson said he had encountered scores of problems like that, which might make no sense to poor, black, and Latino students. "Jerry had to fence his yard, and measure off the distance to know how much piling he needs"—well, said Robinson, I've never had a yard, and haven't seen too many that could be fenced. Students, accordingly, must learn how to remove or replace the variables in a question, and simplify how it is to be imagined.

Classroom methodology, however, is only part of the work since, as Dennis likes to say, there can be no education reform without community reform. In Petersburg mass meetings were routinely held for the benefit of parents. "What is available for their children," said Stella Edwards, who coordinated many of these meetings, "they have no way of knowing, and many won't know until it's too late." The Algebra Project also partnered with Virginia State University, a historically black college located in Petersburg, to bring a dual enrollment program to Petersburg High. Any student who earned a B in Algebra II was given the choice of taking the same calculus course at the high school that is offered at the college, with the credits to be applied to their bachelor degree. The first year it was offered, nine students at Petersburg High took college algebra. All nine passed, and at that point, Dennis said to me, "something happened in this community. It was like, wow, they can do it."

If the Algebra Project, the idea of it, is by itself visionary, in execution it is beholden to the American education complex and all its hazards and bedevilments. One main task of the Algebra Project is the training of teachers. In a district like Petersburg, teachers are constantly tired and under enormous pressure, and they have little time to indulge in creativity when benchmark tests are administered monthly. Every teacher knows they will be collectively scapegoated for a district's failures, making the risk of taking on a novel approach that much greater. Yet they show up; in Petersburg I saw droves filing in for a Saturday morning meeting, and a good chunk of me wondered how they do it. Live the struggle all week, that is, and be back at it Saturday morning, eight a.m. A few even wore shirts that read I GOT IT + YOU GOT IT = MATH SWAGG.

In every district where the Algebra Project launches a program, test scores go up. In 1983 Maisha and the other students Moses had tutored were the first from their school to pass the citywide exam for algebra. Over the next decade, the Algebra Project maintained a presence at the school, and in 1991 its graduates ranked second among Cambridge students in performance on the standardized test. And after two years of the Southern Initiative's tenure, pass rates in Petersburg schools on the Annual Yearly Progress exam in math had risen from 50 to 73 percent.

All the same, the Algebra Project was eventually sent out of Petersburg, when the district's administration changed and voted against continuing the program—a common story of bureaucratic shiftiness and turnover: there are many models aside from the Algebra Project offering relief, and competing claims are made to superintendents and school boards. Dennis can imagine a time—beyond the span of his life though still relatively soon—when charter schools will be regnant, and education will have gone the way of prisons and hospitals and become a private and profitable venture. He points to New Orleans's Recovery School District and what happened there in the years after Hurricane Katrina, when an entire system had to be rebuilt and the new schools were all charter recipients. Students of color, Dennis believes, will be the foil; in cities and the poorest districts education will be converted into a sprawling, lucrative industry, with most performance metrics flatlining or, more probably still, getting worse.

He makes a convincing case, and I cannot think of anything in American life—any utility or public works, any item of our infrastructure—that has not sooner or later been made into big business. Yet it is also possible charter schools are a fad. That's the state of things; everyone in America is hungry for education reform, and cycles happen, and fashions, each generation producing its own retinue of thinkers and strategists, although in a lot of districts—like Petersburg, where accreditation is so rare they hang a banner when it happens—I think the dominant impression is of being divorced from the action and far away from the theorizing of specialists. Call it a public school, a charter or something else. We've still got de facto segregation, miserable dropout rates, wearied teachers and all the rest.

"Our national policy," Moses has said, "is we allow failing schools, but have a policy of rescuing students from failing schools. There are programs designed for different categories"—he meant charter schools, Upward Bound, suburban academies, the whole raft of supplements designed to save public education—"and that lets the country off the hook. Otherwise parents would scream."

He dismissed the idea, but I told Moses I could locate the beginnings of the Algebra Project earlier than anyone—in February 1964, when he granted an interview to Robert Penn Warren, author of *All The King's Men* and the first poet laureate of the United States. Warren visited with Moses for a study he was compiling, published the next year as *Who Speaks for the Negro?*, and wrote: "He thinks that the whole school system, everywhere, aside from the question of race, is failing to meet the needs of the times, that the level of education is the immediate key, not integration as such."

Reading that passage, you have a new sense of the depth of Moses's foresight. He sounds like his mentor, Amzie Moore, for if Moore could see beyond the opening up of lunch counters and bus depots to the centrality of the franchise, Moses knew a desegregation mandate would not automatically raise the quality of education in the poorest schools, and that meant any escape from Jim Crow would be incomplete. Hence Moses's belief that education was always the subtext to the pursuit of voting rights. That was his epiphany—his genius, if you will. He judged more clearly than most the correct nature of the problem, its mass and volume.

When discussing the formation of the Algebra Project, Moses will mention 1944 and those mechanical cotton pickers introduced on the Hopson Plantation. They not only turned thousands of sharecroppers out of their jobs, but signaled the new way, a vast shift in the American economy, one that would materialize over the coming decades. Once centered on labor—on factory and farm work—that economy is now built on technology and computers, the conveyance of information. "In today's world," Moses has said, "economic access and full citizenship depend crucially on math and science literacy." He chose his words carefully; to align a basic facility in math with reading—"literacy"—is to hope people gain a new understanding of the predicament, and grasp its urgency. Math is seen by many as optional, but it isn't, or shouldn't be. Students are removed from the college track if they do not know algebra or trigonometry, and such deficiencies, in any case, rule them out of jobs created by the modern economy. In the lowest-performing districts algebra or math is as much a gateway to the mainstream as learning how to read or count or writing a persuasive term paper.

Moses's entire life, you might say, dramatizes or reveals the complexity of the struggle, and if there is any noble reason for our fascination with him, that is it, though on the other hand maybe the situation is not so complex, and the civil rights movement could be distilled into a single word: access. In Moses's youth, the focus was on gaining entry to restaurants and hotels, and he seized on the vote. He is eighty now, though "the question remains," as he put it, "How do the people in the bottom get into the mix?" For the ways of disempowerment are several. It's more than keeping a slice of the populace away from the ballot box. "They didn't have the citizenship requirements of their age," Moses said of Delta sharecroppers, "and so they were serfs, absolutely without power. What is happening now is that we are watching the new serfs emerge."

Serfs are the product of inferior schools, which function like holding camps in some communities. "The nation doesn't have teachers," Moses said to me. "The nation has no plans to get the teachers it needs. The schools don't have money, and the money they have is not directed to the classrooms, to actually do the work that needs to be done. I've been seeing that now for at least twenty years, and there's no force in the country to move in a different direction."

To contemplate this is to enter a realm of weariness bordering on the benumbing, yet as I told Moses that morning, I'm sure Jim Crow felt that way, and I'm sure all those marches down to the courthouse in McComb felt that way. It's difficult to believe, in other words, that one's sense of fatigue or powerlessness is any greater now than it was fifty years ago. If you got the vote, I told him, you can probably get anything, since what could be tougher than that? But he said the opposite in reply: "Voting was easy compared to education. Because education, at its root in this country, gets down to the issue of where you live, what the family structure is going to be. You might be able to get at it by saying lift these people up and then they can find their own way—but there's no impetus to lift the kids up. There's no real empathy for other people's children."

I remembered what Michael Minor said: when people don't look like you, the sense of togetherness dwindles, becomes harder to maintain. We had now returned to the question that David Dennis had said precipitated Freedom Summer. Whom do we look upon as being the country's children? And if I thought mentioning the lesson of history, those victories of the 1960s, could help temper our resignation, Moses now steered the conversation the other way, and showed me the door to dystopia.

"The metaphor that sustained the country from 1875 to the 1960s was basically white Europeans," he said. "That was the political family of the country. After the sixties that broke up; the symbol of that is the opening up of the Democratic Party and now the election of Barack Obama. But there hasn't been a reconceptualization that has taken root as the American family really is this different kind of family, and it includes this different kind of people as a family, across all the taboos. Absent that, we're in a difficult position with education. The reason we didn't integrate the schools is precisely because the white people didn't want black people as part of their family. They didn't want that to happen, and so it didn't happen. And we're not talking just the South; we're talking all over the country.

"We're in this transition from industrial to information; it's still fluid, but it won't be fluid forever. In your lifetime I think it's going to solidify itself, and if it solidifies itself the way it's going, then the twenty-first-century serfs won't be on plantations. They'll be right in the smack of large urban populations, and it's a crap shoot what will happen—whether people will just be rounding them up and throwing them away into prisons, helter skelter."

3.

The Mississippi Summer Project is a Trojan horse; I spent years not understanding it, or not really seeing it for what it was. To this day I dislike the way history has preserved or perpetuates the Summer Project's mission. If back then it was all about the whites, to a large degree it still is. When people know Freedom Summer at all it is usually because of the June 21 murders—many have seen *Mississippi Burning*—and those murders are infamous chiefly because two of the victims were white. As authorities dredged the state's rivers looking for the bodies of Chaney, Goodman, and Schwerner, they found other bodies, black ones, like those of Henry Dee and Charles Moore, who were killed in May 1964, and others unnamed or too disfigured to be identified. Yet these murders are forgotten. Fifty years on, there is still an imbalance, a skewing of emphasis; history and the past show the same face.

I thought that the Summer Project held the mind for all the wrong reasons, and I tried to stay away from it, insofar as I could. But I could not leave it alone forever, my subject matter being what it is, and as I began to interview Freedom Summer volunteers I noticed something significant: most of them shared my reservations. They did not want to be valorized; Kirschenbaum, for instance, told me his hosts had put themselves on the line in a way he never could: "We lived with a family named Colley, and Mr. and Mrs. Colley—and that's all we ever called them, we were probably the first white people who ever addressed them as Mr.

and Mrs.——had six children and three bedrooms, and they gave up one of those bedrooms so that Fred, who was an African American Chicago college student, and I shared one and somehow the eight of them occupied the other two. We contributed to groceries; they accepted no money. And they were the real heroes. Mrs. Colley woke up every morning at four or five a.m., got the children ready for school, and would go off for work at a shipyard in Pascagoula, where she loaded sixty-pound tuna from the boats. Mr. Colley was a carpenter. Two people who were willing to risk it all. I don't know if they did anything beyond allow us to stay there—but that was major."

It is not widely known, but white college students had traveled to Mississippi the year before too, at the behest of Allard Lowenstein, a former dean at Stanford and faculty member at Yale. Lowenstein was a veteran of the left. In 1959 he had visited the territory of South-West Africa, what is now Namibia, then under South African rule. He witnessed an unusual practice: though it was illegal under apartheid for Africans to engage in political activity, they staged mock elections, finely detailed test runs. Memory of that returned to Lowenstein four years later, when he went to Mississippi and sought out Moses. Most of the COFO staff, Moses reported, was wary and desperate, "butting their heads up against a stone wall, with no breakthroughs," and he was intrigued by the notion of a mock ballot. It was an election year, and if they could get it together in time, COFO could mimic the state's electoral calendar, educating the citizenry on protocol without having to worry about the sheriff in the courthouse or the names of registrants being shared in the local paper, people getting evicted from their homes and inciting the marauding of the Klan. And the simulation would be an important symbolic move, hugely needed at a time when many white Mississippians alleged blacks had no interest in entering politics or winning the ballot, that they were happy with the current scheme of things.

Preparations for the Freedom Vote took place in the late summer and fall of 1963. For help Lowenstein recruited almost a hundred students from those universities—such as Stanford and Yale—where he had connections. A convention was held at the Masonic Temple in Jackson; candidates for governor and lieutenant governor were nominated, and more than eighty thousand ballots cast, collected at churches and black-owned business, secret, out-of-the-way places. In a report on the campaign Dennis wrote: "Many people felt that this was silly and was some sort of plaything, but, on the contrary, it did much more for the movement, toward uniting Mississippi, than anything else we have done."

The freedom ballot led to the establishment of a political party, the Mississippi Freedom Democratic Party. The name identified it as an alternative to the state's Democratic contingent, which held every one of Mississippi's congressional seats and was of course all white. If 1963 featured a race for governor, 1964 brought one for president. The movement planned to reenact the Freedom Vote, only this time it would not be kept secret. At the end of Freedom Summer the Mississippi Freedom Democratic Party would send its own delegates to the National Convention in Atlantic City; that was the mountain the Summer Project was acted out against, and moved ever closer to. In Atlantic City they would formally protest the legitimacy of the state's delegation, calling attention to voter suppression in the most public of forums, allowing the rest of the country to stand in judgment.

The Freedom Democratic Party gave volunteers like Kirschenbaum a secondary purpose. They signed up very few new voters that summer. In Panola County in the northern part of the state, federal overseers had been able to strip the voter application of all interpretive questions, like those concerning the state constitution, the ones that traditionally had been used to turn away black applicants. More than eight hundred African Americans, as a result, signed up to vote in Panola County. And that was twice as many as in the rest of the state. If you were stationed somewhere else, then what you got was the standard Mississippi experience, where suspense had to do not with whether you would help anyone register but rather which type of contumely you were subject to. Unlike in years past, however, in the face of resistance volunteers could enroll residents in the Freedom Democratic Party and discuss Atlantic City and primary procedure.

But canvassing, it should be remembered, was only one aspect of the work. Volunteers set up community centers and what became known as freedom schools, where civics was taught, and creative writing. These schools—like the class on Johns Island—had a curriculum unlike any the South had ever seen. Kirschenbaum asked the students in Moss Point to write "simple stories" in the manner of Langston Hughes, and sent them to the poet, who mailed a note of thanks to every child. Mark Levy, another New Yorker, taught in the freedom school in Meridian, and could not figure out why the students wanted to learn French and typing above all else—until they told him it was because those were the subjects taught in the white part of town. The history of the civil rights movement was reviewed, as were African American contributions to music and literature. Although the transaction, ultimately, was probably more impactful on the other side. Lewis Hyde, the author, among other books, of the classic treatise *The Gift: Creativity and the Artist in the Modern World*, spent the summer of 1964 in Laurel, Mississippi. Of the freedom school there he recalled: "We taught Negro history, but I didn't know this history. When I grew up in Pittsburgh I took English classes. Nobody ever taught a slave narrative in the 1960s. In a funny way the white folk from the North were teaching it to themselves as well as to those kids."

Alongside the Freedom Democratic Party and the schools, many lawyers and doctors had also chosen to spend the summer in Mississippi. The Summer Project had it all, and the idea was revolutionary when you think about it, but also supremely logical. Since Mississippi would not admit blacks into the mainstream, the movement decided to create its own state, a rival or shadow body that maintained its own model of politics and teaching, offering its participants health care, legal counsel, and even worship, for a bevy of pastors and rabbis joined the Freedom Summer ranks as well. It was an unprecedented assembly. During debates held early in the year about whether or not the movement should open itself up to white involvement on this scale, Moses had said, "I always thought that the one thing we can do for the country that no one else can do is to be above the race issue." Freedom Summer connected every stratum of American life; pick your dichotomy—rich and poor, black and white, North and South, urban and rural— and they all mingled for those hundred days, in a way, to my mind, that hasn't been seen since. The arrangement no doubt created its share of tension, and awkward, even confrontational moments— but remember what the Summer Project was. It was a gesture to the rest of the country. It was not a utopia.

It was also a brief installation; in August 1964 it attempted to merge with the rest of America—or the opposite, and make the rest of America accommodate its demands—and that could not be done. The Freedom Party's challenge at the Democratic National Convention was defeated. Their delegates were not recognized but, thanks to Lyndon Johnson's cajoling, offered a pair of token seats on the floor. Evidently none of the Summer Project's leaders had prepared for the possibility. They were ready only for victory, and refused the offer. Many in the movement, believing the federal government had placed its weight against them once and for all, fell into a stupor. Moses and Dennis dropped out. James Forman, the head of SNCC, proposed a sequel to the Summer Project, one that would be staged across all of the black belt region of the South, but internal division wiped out the plan. SNCC's anxieties over white involvement could no longer be contained; for many of its members, the new doctrine of "Black Power" forbade any form of interracial alliance, and the organization chose to dismiss the whites among its staff. It didn't take long for the Summer Project to be viewed as an anachronism, the folly of an earlier and more naïve time. Moses told me it was easy to forget about in Africa because everyone he knew there, men and women of a militant persuasion, with a passionate belief in black unity, considered Freedom Summer a joke.

Over the following decades he came back to it—gradually—and now regards Freedom Summer as an essential piece in the story of America. Moses tells that story like no other. His version is a cyclical tale, framed by the rhetoric of the Constitution.

> We have to reconceptualize the understanding of the Freedom Riders, the sit-in movement, the sharecroppers, the voting rights movement, not as the struggle of black people, but as the struggle of a people to reassert the meaning of "We the People," the meaning of a constitutional person, and the meaning of that was that they were citizens of a nation, not citizens of Mississippi and Alabama and so forth, and that being a citizen of a nation means something and trumps state personhood. But to do that people can't think of themselves as, well, we are white people, we are black people, we are this kind of people. And it's difficult, because the idea of a constitutional person is abstract, but the Constitution is the only thing that actually binds everybody together; it's the glue for the country, and so people have to own it.
>
> We're the levers for change. And it's interesting, Roberts and the Supreme Court is in the process of constructing a framework of the feds versus the states and resurrecting the concept of states' rights. But if you look at the history of the country, there were always three

forces: there were the feds, there were the states—but there were also various manifestations of "We the People." The first were described in the *Dred Scott* decision. Taney really describes the idea of the political family, white men who worked with the feds around their interest, and their basic interest was property, land and slaves, and they worked with the feds to get their land and to ensure that runaway property came back.

The civil rights movement, what emerged was a really powerful impetus from the black movement itself, which in the case of Mississippi Freedom Summer, the March on Washington, Birmingham, called on the larger population as a manifestation of "We the People," and so you got, again, that kind of manifestation working with the feds against the states to enlarge not constitutional statehood, but constitutional personhood. This is the tension that is built into the country; it's there from the beginning. What is lacking today is "We the People." There's not a force that is needed to work with the feds against all these other various groups, and part of the problem, particularly around education, is there's not a political force that has an interest in the people we're reaching. Obama and the whole Democratic crowd are really in hock to the elite forces, money forces. We don't have any kind of grassroots politics.

It may not sound like it, but this is a call for a movement, as clarion as what John Perdew said to me in his home in Atlanta. Grassroots politics cannot come to life on its own, and the role of an organizer, when Moses describes it, sounds like that of a missionary: "You're in an organizing mode when you are working with some other people to get them to do something that you cannot do yourself." It was no good for field secretaries to go to Mississippi and say, give them the vote. Until the locals voiced the demand it was meaningless. Change—particularly when we are talking about the poor and people of color—can never occur without pressure, and the pressure must be made by those who stand to benefit from better, more equable treatment. And so you work the demand side, as Moses says, try to make the demand louder, the strategy providing yet another connection between the past and today, between the vote and education. It explains what happened on Johns Island and throughout the rest of the Low Country. And the year after those nine students passed the dual enrollment algebra course at Petersburg High, forty-four requested admission into the same class. No one had recruited them; they asked to be let in on their own, and soon parents were asking about dual enrollment at mass meetings, the prospect of their child attending college having suddenly become a lot more manageable. "To me," said Dennis, "that's how you measure success."

I told Moses I couldn't think of anything more hopeful than working the demand side, because the technique is predicated on a faith the demand will be met, no matter how imperfectly or belatedly. It's an assent, intentional or otherwise, to the American democratic process. But I thought of something else too—of Moses's favorite quotation by Ella Baker, an organizer who informed so much of his philosophy about the movement, whom he shared long talks with during that formative summer of 1960. It runs: "In order for us as poor and oppressed people to become a part of a society that is meaningful, the system under which we now exist has to be radically changed."

So which is it, I asked: change the present structure or move within it, cultivating demand?

"You can also work the demand side," went his answer, "because that's what you can do."

"You can't do that, what she's talking about?"

"I'm not sure how—I don't run across the people that have a

clue about how that gets done. I'm not saying it couldn't be done; I just don't have a clue about how it gets done."

"So you work the demand side to stay in the realm of the possible?"

"To stay within the realm of the sane."

And that was the only time in all of our conversations that Moses smiled.

———

The Mississippi Summer Project is a Trojan horse, and why? Because it baits you into focusing on the lure of violence and the students being used as pawns. Yet hidden inside is the answer, or one answer. Freedom Summer said to Mississippi and the rest of America: if you do not let us in then we will do it ourselves; we can beget and administer our own systems. We can go our own way, and that creates a third choice. Beyond any attempts at reform or working to stretch the law to its maximum elasticity, there is also this example of parallel institutions. And if 1964 used to be something to forget about, today Moses sees it as something to repeat.

"I don't know where it will come or who will step into it, somebody who becomes the public face of the issues we are talking about. If you just think of the Summer Project, the coming together of all those people for that brief moment—the students, the teachers, the lawyers—they came together as a manifestation of 'We the People.' There was nothing that could hold them all together and say this manifestation needs to keep working, and figure out how to keep working. That was not going to happen. But it did come together. And it was clear you needed to have that; you couldn't move the country with just the SNCC people and the black people in Mississippi. You needed the country in its larger sense to assemble—to move itself."

"That's the only way it gets done," I said, and he answered: "I

171

think that's what the history tells us. I look at the country in three-quarters-of-a-century chunks. From 1787 to the 1860s, there's the national government, which becomes strong because it has all this land from the Appalachians to the Rockies that it owns and can sell. It's the national government and these white men, the constitutional people; and the states and the constitutional property, the slaves. They fall out with each other, and there's a big reckoning, but they get reconciled and we go for another three-quarters of a century, in which it's the same family and the people who are descendants of the freed slaves are into Jim Crow. The only thing that breaks that is this emergence of another manifestation of 'We the People.' So that's been the history of how the country has lurched forward and backward; it lurched forward, then lurched back, then lurched forward again, is lurching back. It did that the first two times roughly every seventy-five years, and we're sort of two-thirds of the way through our third three-quarters of a century. So it's conceivable that this manifestation of 'We the People' might reemerge. I look at the generation that's from ten and forty now; they might actually figure out they don't want to live this way, we want to live *this way*, and pull themselves together. And they would have to figure out how to reconfigure the metaphor of the American family."

It was a complex vision that he articulated, deterministic on the one hand, saying the country was bound to these cycles, seventy-five-year weather patterns, but also stating, on the other, that we have some election over which way it will go. And he's right: there's only one mass that can settle these questions. Moses and Dennis, their time is almost up. It will all have to be decided by the young people—the children of the country.

4.

When flying into Miami or Fort Lauderdale it is easy to believe one has left the South behind. A new kind of landscape is below, dotted with jungle flora and bejeweled, the shimmer of rooftop and backyard pool contributing to a glare that is curtailed only by the shoreline. The city seems poised at a precarious point, for the little canals and intercoastals that stitch the neighborhoods together may, for all the visitor knows, be the receding waters of a flood, threatening at any time to swell back and swallow up the strip malls and subdivisions. A different clientele waits in the airport than what you find in Memphis or Birmingham or Jackson. The vacationers and cruise hoppers, they have been delivered, at least temporarily, and order margaritas on the flight down, laugh and exclaim liberally as they rise and move toward the jetway, yet those who have relocated here display a restless and darting quality, as though they have come to the end of things, flown deep into this peninsular appendage of America only to find it not what they imagined, not the end of things at all but a continuation, a reordering possibly, but still full of whatever it is they cannot shuck.

And soon, as one drives out of the terminal past palm trees, the frail or diseased ones kept in place by wooden supports, familiarity and routine begin to reassert themselves. The palm trees may even be necessary, now, to remind one of the locale. In Miami as everywhere else the interstate was run through the black neighborhoods, so the ghetto or inner city or whatever the prevailing term of choice sits close, within earshot, of the I-95 overpasses. The housing projects, built in mandarin and pastel shades, look blank and abandoned, though socks, towels and sheets are hung on the lines. Outside the barred windows of a convenience store a few take off their shirts in the sultry air. Others sit hunched, in prayerful attitudes, beneath the arcing, cane-like shelters erected at bus stations.

Liberty City, as this particular section of north Miami is called, may seem somnolent on a weekday morning, but it boiled over in May 1980 after the acquittal of four police officers charged with manslaughter following the death of Arthur McDuffie, an African American insurance agent. One night McDuffie, who was riding his motorcycle with a suspended license, was observed running a stoplight. He briefly eluded the officers at high speed. When he surrendered, he was handcuffed with a baton under his chin and beaten to death, his skull cracked by the blows of a flashlight handle. The police tried—in vain—to make his death look like an accident; they broke the legs of McDuffie's corpse, drove the squad car over his motorcycle and bashed the pavement with a tire iron to show where the bike, in their description of events, crashed. To avoid controversy or violence the trial was moved to Tampa, and on May 17, 1980, twelve whites returned with a decision of not guilty. Rioting lasted for three days after the verdict was announced. Later, a study that was commissioned found the melee in Liberty City to be fundamentally different from those that happened in Newark and Watts in the 1960s. One had to go back to the slave uprisings of the nineteenth century to find a precedent, it was said, since the violence that was loosed, with eighteen murdered and several others beaten, was purposeful and not, as in Newark or Watts, a corollary of looting and arson. Liberty City—like Philadelphia, Mississippi—was given a scarlet letter, a trademark, and that is what accounts for the peculiar disconnect that exists between the reputation of so many of these places and their residents. Though many in Liberty City have no idea who Arthur McDuffie was, whenever it is mentioned in the popular media some description of the 1980 riots will inevitably follow.

The Dream Defenders, a group of seven activists all of whom are in their twenties, move in various senses within the shadow of Arthur McDuffie. Their offices are located on the other side of I-95 from Liberty City, and most of their activity concentrates on police brutality, on the impunity and abandon with which African Americans are arrested or killed. The Dream Defenders will always be associated with Trayvon Martin, for it was in April 2012 that two of them, Phillip Agnew and Ahmad Abuznaid, decided to hold a conference call. They had met years before, as members of the fraternity that founded a Student Coalition for Justice in Tallahassee. At that time Agnew was vice president of the student body at Florida A&M, and Abuznaid held the same title at Florida State. Now they hoped to find a way of pressuring the police in Sanford, Florida, into arresting George Zimmerman, who had admitted to shooting Martin but claimed he had done so in self-defense.

Details of the call were shared over Facebook, and they were ultimately joined by 150 others. One caller had gone to Selma the month before for the annual crossing of the Edmund Pettus Bridge that commemorates Bloody Sunday. She suggested an action on that scale, so they marched. Fifty college students and alums of the Student Coalition for Justice, in imitation of what had transpired in Selma and going under the ad hoc name Dream Defenders— someone else on the call had mentioned Dr. King's speech at the March on Washington, its promise of universal brotherhood— spent three days walking from Daytona to Sanford. When they arrived at the police station they kneeled in front of the entrance, called for Zimmerman's arrest, and also demanded the resignation of the chief of police. By the end of the week, amid what amounted to a national uproar, both of these things had happened.

"Everyone who was a part of that march decided this could

not be a one-time action," Abuznaid told me. "It needed to be a sustained process. So that's when our Dream Defenders became an organization."

They spent the rest of 2012 hosting retreats, recruiting members and rearranging their lives. Curtis Hierro, their field director, dropped out of graduate school—but not before taking out a large student loan. Until recently, when they moved into that office in North Miami, business was conducted in living rooms and coffee shops. The clocks have been rewound, in other words, to show if not quite zero then a span only minimally past the starting point. Interviewing Robert Moses or David Dennis is a different kind of enterprise: when you do that you hope to isolate a path leading up to where you are now, to sort out a form from all the detritus of fifty years. To enter the Dream Defenders' office—a dim room with a dry-erase board and a series of padded abutments that mark a row of desks—is to face the other direction, what looks like a virginal expanse and shows no print, no sign of traffic. They are a group that has been forced to define themselves and resolve questions of form and strategy in a time much shorter than what might ordinarily be allotted. Decisions are made on the fly, with occasional recourse to guesswork, as befits a shotgun affair.

Once the group came together, Agnew was named executive director. He is not from Florida but Chicago, raised by devout parents who assembled a meager income through secondhand book sales. Agnew's father acquired titles at thrift stores and brought them to the flea market every Thursday and Sunday. In the days between, Agnew would steal into the garage, where the books were kept, and read, even as he was being taught about the gospel at dinnertime. He was constantly moving between the two worlds, the separate realms of the word, and became an imaginative and introspective teen, albeit one with a determination not to be poor. After graduating from Florida A&M, he worked in sales for a large pharmaceutical company. Two weeks after the march to Sanford he quit and moved into Abuznaid's house in Miami, where the earliest plans for the Dream Defenders were being drafted. "We were all there together," he said. "It was like a *Real World* house."

It's no small task to set up an organization with only a minimum of funding, and the reason the Dream Defenders have had to work on the fly, resolving questions of identity and protocol as they go, is that in the summer of 2013 they occupied the capital in Florida for one month. It was the longest demonstration Tallahassee had ever witnessed, and incipient though the group was, they now acquired a national reputation, becoming subject of one feature after another and earning praise from the likes of Harry Belafonte and Talib Kweli. They may not have expected all the attention that came their way, but they capitalized on it, and took the chance of representing themselves as the way forward. "We are a movement for a new generation," Hierro was quoted in the *New York Times* report on the sit-in.

The genesis of the demonstration was similar to what had occurred the previous spring. Zimmerman's acquittal was read on the night of July 13, 2013. Agnew and Abuznaid got on the phone with their friends from the Student Coalition for Justice and learned that a march was set to take place in Tallahassee; they decided to drive up from Miami, and as they did they lighted on the idea of going to the capitol. They had done that once before, staging a sit-in near the governor's office in 2006 after a teenager, Martin Lee Anderson, died in a juvenile boot camp, the victim of abuse by guards. The plan was reprised, and on Tuesday, July 16, a group of protestors moved into the hallway outside the office of governor Rick Scott. A few said they would stay and spend the night if necessary, waiting until they were granted an audience. Their intention was modest: they wanted Scott to call a special session of the legislature to review Stand Your Ground, the law made infamous by the death of Martin, which makes it legal for anyone who senses a threat—who fears injury or death—to defend themselves even when escape is possible. In addition to muddying the question of self-defense, Stand Your Ground would seem to encourage the belief that to pose a threat is to commit a crime. And black men in America do not have to do much, or anything at all, to be viewed as a threat. "They weren't the most radical demands," Agnew said. "We weren't calling for anybody's head; we were calling for a genuine discussion about a law that was horribly written and disproportionately applied and resulted in many of the jury instructions that allow for somebody"—he meant Zimmerman, of course—"to get off for killing a kid."

After forty-eight hours, Scott agreed to meet with them. Chairs were arranged in a circle in his office and five Dream Defenders shown in. He was polite to start with, though after introductions were made he crossed his legs and revealed a pair of black leather boots decorated with small flag designs. One of the protestors commented on his footwear. "Oh, for all you history buffs," he said, lifting a heel, "What are the different flags that have flown over the state of Florida?" And he pointed out the banners of Spain and Florida as well as Dixie. Scott is from Illinois originally—he ran a hospital conglomerate and made millions of dollars before entering politics—but he nevertheless felt compelled, in this setting, to expound on what the stars and bars meant to him, why he cherishes the doctrine of states' rights that flag is said to embody.

The rest of the meeting, as it played out, was perfunctory. Scott said he had sent his condolences to the family of Trayvon Martin and urged them to contact the Department of Education and his Department of Justice secretary. Every possibility for reform, he promised, would be reviewed, and then—and nothing can summarize the Southern Tea Partier quite like this detail—he suggested they all pray together.

The Dream Defenders said they had no choice but to continue the sit-in, and over the next few weeks plenty of reinforcements would arrive, buses of supporters pulling up from New

York, Philadelphia, and Baltimore. Some would stay in the capital for a night or two, be spelled by another for that same duration and return. No arrests were made—the state was shrewd for that—and by and by the protest acquired the forms of habit. Occupants were forbidden from carrying an air mattress or anything else that might qualify as a fire hazard, so at night they laid thin mats across the capitol's cool ground floor. They woke at five to begin cleaning up; breakfast was delivered daily—eggs usually, with a side of grits and toast—and had returned to the hall outside Scott's office when the capital opened at eight. While much of America was in thrall to the symbolic power of the event, the reason the Dream Defenders stayed as long as they did, thirty-one days and thirty nights, was because that was the amount of time they spent lobbying for the special session.

"We left because strategically we had exhausted all of our options," Agnew told me. "When we came there on day one, it was to get a special session of the legislature. There are three ways for that to happen. The first way is the governor can call for a special session. That way was exhausted by the third day. The second way is you do a poll of the legislature and they call for a special session; the only way that you can get a poll triggered is if you get a certain amount of senators and representatives to say they want a poll. We were able to trigger that through a whole lot of phone calls and politicking and were actually the first group not represented by a lawmaker to trigger the poll for a special session. That failed because we have a Republican-led legislature. The third way is for the Speaker of the House or the Senate President to do it, and we thought we were making some inroads there. About the twenty-ninth day or the thirtieth day we found we had reached an impasse; some political interests had moved and they weren't budging. We decided we got to get out of here; there's only so much we can do from inside this building. Our movements were restricted there; our conversations had to be washed over. It wasn't the best place to start strategizing. A lot of folks wanted us to stay a little longer, and we just couldn't. At some point you've got to move on to the next tactic."

After they left the Dream Defenders began to field calls from all over the country and found that, while they still regarded themselves as an underground or fledgling organization, no one else did. Requests were made to start a new chapter in this city or that, yet there was no outline in place, no set of procedures or blueprint that could be shared, for what it means to be a Dream Defender is not a question that has been entirely decided. They seem certain, however, their focus will rest on criminalization, on dismantling what seems after a while like a self-fulfilling prophecy, as African Americans are not only viewed as criminals but can each be made into one rather easily, and it's not just the War on Drugs anymore, with mandatory sentencing and the elevation of certain crimes into the felony category. Each year the distinction between schools and the criminal justice system becomes vaguer and vaguer. Students in cities like Miami and Oakland confront a nightmarish reality, as if conjured by some fabulist, Kafka or Borges, where schools have been made to resemble penal colonies, overcrowded, with cops roaming the halls and metal detectors placed at the entrance, a line painted down the center of the floor that one must follow, single-file, and the principals like wardens, concerned with discipline first and last, and looking for ways to stretch the budget and accommodate more guards. In many districts one can be expelled or arrested for a petty offense, dabbling with pot, say, or quarreling with a classmate, and end up in a juvenile detention center or on the street, contemplating the merits of gang initiation. This is what is known as "the school-to-prison pipeline," and experts like to point out it only runs one way. There is no prison-to-school pipeline.

"The twenty-first-century serfs," Robert Moses had said, "won't be on plantations. They'll be right in the smack of large urban populations, and it's a crap shot what will happen—whether people will just be rounding them up and throwing them away into prisons, helter skelter." People do have to go to jail, of course, and often for legitimate reasons, though that's also where the money is, and the political clout. In the summer of 2014, as his reelection campaign was getting under way, Scott held a fundraiser at the residence of George Zoley, a founder of the GEO group, a private manufacturer of prisons. The annual revenue of the GEO group exceeds a billion dollars. Admission to the party at Zoley's compound in Boca Raton was steep, with tickets listed at $3,000, or $10,000 for a place in the "VIP reception with photo opportunity."

To go up against that, you might say, is tantamount to taking on Nike or Coca-Cola, and the Dream Defenders understand that while it is well and good to stage a march, a wider education must also take place. "So this is black community politics right now," said Steven Pargett, their director of communications. "Something happens, somebody gets shot, and then Jesse Jackson or Al Sharpton goes to that city and there's a one-day march and everybody stops talking about it. I'm twenty-five. I didn't grow up in the world where Malcolm X or Stokely Carmichael or SNCC were real things that I could see, or that people around me were directly influenced by because it was a part of the culture. Rather, I grew up in a world that those were things in books, and maybe a documentary if you searched for it, and they certainly didn't teach us about, like, civil disobedience, nonviolent direct action, anything like that. They didn't really teach you to be an engaged or involved citizen in school; that's not what school's about. So our role as Dream Defenders is not only to pick battles around issues and win on issues but to define what it means to be a young person of color and be involved in the movement; to redefine what the movement is and how you can participate in it; to do campaigns and win, but we have to show people what all of this looks like to a generation that it wasn't a real thing."

Pargett, whose hair is dreadlocked, is fit and of medium height, and the inflections of his voice tend to be more animated than his calm and studious disposition. Like Agnew he went to Florida A&M—but never graduated. He was too busy, he says, and got overextended, founding a start-up while also serving as campus liaison for the AFL-CIO and participating in Occupy. He learned of the Dream Defenders by attending a retreat in Miami, and initially he hoped to convince them to pursue a concert series. For part of the redefinition he was describing had to do with the cultural engagement of the movement.

"Hip-hop," he said, "is really important when you're looking at urban communities. Hip-hop is the story of an industry with multiple business empires built literally from nothing, from the foundation of a couple guys standing on the corner and talking shit and then they started to rhyme and then they started to do it in a club. It's an art form that requires little materials. In fact hip-hop comes from a place where they were taking a lot of musical instruments out of schools."

As he laid out this creation myth, I thought of the Delta and how the blues evolved there a century ago, a man and his guitar, this mythical dyad traceable to the fact that drums were banned on many of the plantations, forcing the rhythmic impulse to seek expression through other means.

"We just went to Jamaica," he went on. "One of the really hot songs right now is 'Hot Nigga.' It's got this dance, the Shmoney dance, because the guy's name is Bobby Shmurda. And the song is crap, he's just talking about killing people and selling drugs, but everybody loves the dance, and that's why everybody loves the song. After hearing a bunch of dance-hall and reggae and all that, it was awesome at the end of the night, when the DJ's really turning up, he plays 'Hot Nigga' and there's a thousand Jamaicans doing the Shmoney dance, and it's like: 'Damn, look at how powerful this culture is.' And they also have CNN and they're influenced by the news—but that's the mainstream media, and we can't create that. We cannot get behind the reins of that."

Pargett's view of hip-hop not only harkened back to origin myths but was post-lapsarian as well. "It was deeply rooted in politics," he told me, "and there's light showing it can be like that again, which it got away from in this age of gangsta rap."

"Are you talking about Public Enemy?" I said. Pargett replied:

Yeah, like Public Enemy, "Fight the Power," and "Fight the Power" not only being an anthem but being in a Spike Lee movie so that everybody was introduced to it. There's a lot more cool stuff coming out now. In the wake of Mike Brown being murdered,* a bunch of megastars came together and made a song called "Don't Shoot": the Game, 2 Chainz, Diddy, Rick Ross, Problem, a bunch of R&B singers. And with the misogyny and patriarchy it's really hard to have a relationship between hip-hop and a progressive political movement. There's two of us behind the Twitter right now. One, Ciara, is having a really progressive conversation, Women in 2014 I think is the hashtag, and then I saw this awesome Childish Gambino interview, I put it on there, somebody tweets us back: Why are you elevating these rappers that make jokes about raping women? I don't know what they're talking about; I don't know what interview or what song that was in. It's so difficult. It's not perfect, it's not politically correct, but it is where a lot of people are at, and that's where the opportunity is, because people aren't progressive, people don't know what the fuck the

---

* Michael Brown was an African American teenager killed by a police officer in Ferguson, Missouri, on August 9, 2014. Brown was unarmed, and though eyewitness accounts of his killing differ, many claimed he had raised his arms in surrender before being shot.

school-to-prison pipeline is, people don't know any of these statistics. Only thirty-thousand people follow us on Twitter; there's millions of people on Twitter. We're by no means in the public lexicon of black and brown young people right now, so how do we meet them halfway?

You don't have to take the risk of affiliating with an organization. Just talk about the issue. When Jay-Z performed at the Rose Bowl all he said was, "Build more schools, less prisons," but that's all organizations like us needs to go and run with it. That's a press release for somebody. Getting a video on World Star Hip Hop would be a huge deal for us. We've tried. That site gets millions of viewers from what we say is our base every single day. Getting a video that's popping on World Star Hip Hop would mean more than getting on MSNBC. Apparel is another opportunity. If Dream Defenders co-brands a line that's promoted on the top banner of karmaloop.com, that would be a huge deal. After Mike Brown is murdered—there's a site called teespring, and teespring is basically a way to run a crowd-funding campaign where all people do is purchase T-shirts or apparel. We start selling DON'T SHOOT shirts and it took off. We tried to sell a hundred, we sold over 1,300 and raised 15,000 dollars. On the third day, John Legend does a performance on yahoo live and he's wearing a DON'T SHOOT shirt, and while he's performing the news editor for *Vanity Fair* is like, hey, if you like John Legend's T-shirt, you can get yours from the Dream Defenders. It's so indirect, but still, if the movement has messaging and that messaging can be put on a T-shirt and you can just rock the shirt, it may not be the most powerful statement, but it's at least like a hat-tip that a lot of people will get.

And that's why it has to be cool, man. If there's a

hype moment that everybody's paying attention to, they might listen for right then, but they're not going to listen two days later. It really has to be a movement; it has to feel like something that has space for you.

———

The need for it to be cool was a recurring topic that day, a motto of sorts, delivered with equal parts irony and sincerity. Even as he told me this, Pargett was finalizing the details of a block party sponsored by the organization to take place during homecoming at Florida A&M, one of the most popular events in the state. And Hierro, the Dream Defenders' field director, told me, "In the non-profit world we get in this little bubble, but people want to go to the club, right? People like short, powerful slogans; people like Kanye West—well, some people do. I like Kanye West. So how are we tapping into the cultural climate that's there? You could critique it, but you got to reach people where they're at. So yeah, you got to be cool. Or try. I'm trying."

Hierro's father is Cuban. He emigrated to Miami during the famous Mariel boat lift and became involved in the cocaine trade, serving, Hierro said, as "a mid-management enforcer type." He can remember staying in a hotel room that was raided, and after his father was sent to jail he drifted in and out of homelessness before ending up in Orlando, where other members of his family had moved in the aftermath of Hurricane Andrew. Hierro attended Central Florida and was planning an academic career when in 2009 he began to advocate for the DREAM Act[*] and farmworkers'

———

[*] Legislation whose name stands for Development, Relief, and Education of Alien Minors. Introduced in the Senate in 2001 and debated again by Congress in 2010 and 2011, the DREAM Act sets forth ways for undocumented immigrants who have graduated from a U.S. high school to attain citizenship status.

rights. "That was my introduction to organizing," he said, "and I loved it, loved the sense of community, but also the conflict, seeing how you can confront power directly, growers, corporations, elected officials." Later he joined the campaign of congressman Alan Grayson, only to discover he hated politics, and left to establish a Dream Defenders chapter in Orlando. He possesses a theoretical turn of mind—the academic inclination comes through at once—and of the seven who comprise the core staff, he is the one whose view is conditioned most by history.

"There's a whole field of study called civil resistance," he told me, "and academics like Erica Chenoweth and others have looked at history and found an interesting phenomenon: when 3.5 percent of a population is actively involved in a movement, that movement achieves victory.* It's been universal the past fifty years—3.5 percent. We're a country of what, 300 million people? What if we got 3.5 percent—which is still a pretty large number—to be actively engaged, voting, not cooperating with certain entities? You could see a mass change, right?

"We're still figuring out the best structure for the organization, how we start to pollinate; people every day have been like, 'I want to start a Dream Defenders chapter,' and we've been, 'Well no, we got to perfect it here in Florida first.' I've been studying organizing intensively for the past five years but especially the last year—specifically two trends. You have the structure-based trend, best personified by a lot of labor unions, the old Acorn network, Saul Alinsky style: run strict local campaigns, very incremental approach, like you organize around streetlights. There's another trend, and you've seen this in the American civil rights movement: the momentum tradition. Moving tons of people and creating dilemma actions, so like the sit-in at the Sanford police station: are

---

* Chenoweth explores this theory in her book *Why Civil Resistance Works*, written with Maria J. Stephan.

you going to arrest us or George Zimmerman? Either way they lose, you let us stay or you arrest us and look like the villain. It was like this is a moment of crisis: how do we create a dilemma for the people responsible?"

Hierro imagined the Dream Defenders binding these traditions and wedding the movement's twin strains of organizing and civil disobedience, and all I could think was: yes, the clocks really have been reset, for this was like returning to the earliest days of SNCC, when a similar plan was laid out in McComb and Moses put in charge of voter registration, while Marion Barry was appointed to oversee boycotts and other forms of direct action. Pargett had provided a glimpse of something new, with his talk of hip-hop and fashion and Jay-Z replacing "This Little Light of Mine," but in Hierro's plan I could see something like a familiar shape, evidence of the movement as a continuum. This came out too when I spoke with Jonel Edwards, who directs the Dream Defenders' activity in Florida's northern half, between Orlando and Tallahassee. "I'm really interested in parallel institutions," she told me, "opening a community bank, or opening a community school. We talk about reforming things, but we don't talk enough about creating things."

Fifty years had transpired between Freedom Summer and the conversation we were having now, and all the statistics and theory aside, maybe there can be no greater indictment of the present than that plain and irrefutable fact. The citizenship schools, the freedom schools: she was formulating a similar plan, and instead of waiting for the state to provide thought it better to break away, for the Dream Defenders to work to the point where such an option—the establishment of a school that set its own rules and curriculum—would at least be possible. Not to reform but to create, that was the dialectic, the eternal push-and-pull of denial leading to invention, like Pargett's story of hip-hop beginning the moment instruments were taken away. The problems would endure, and life would have the feel, many days, of a treadmill, with much effort and little progress, yet the invention would also endure, the movement constantly dreaming up reality's counterstroke and looking for ways to bring this otherness into being. And in that regard the Dream Defenders were charged with more than just their stated aim of galvanizing the young and altering the fate of the cities. They had to grow, yes, but without becoming tame or domesticated, and what they wanted was somehow to pull off the paradoxical thing and implement a system that is no system but remains where the movement must, on the margins and uncontained, a permanent outlier.

"One of the most interesting phenomenons we've seen in the past twenty years," Hierro, their resident historian, told me, "is the growth of the open-source movement, represented by groups like Anonymous, the Pirate Party in Europe, where essentially you create a DNA of your organization and then you let it go. Train lots of people, this is how you organize, these are the possible campaigns you can run, and let it go and create little wildfires across the United States. Other organizations, you got to go up the bureaucracy to get something approved. What we're saying is, if you have an idea and we've trained you, it fits within the parameters of the organization—it's nonviolent, and part of our grand strategy to empower our people—you can do it. And the best ideas will rise to the top. Because people will vote with their feet. They'll say that's a good idea, I'm going to do it; or they won't.

"And that's how we think we can stay at the cusp of innovating the young folks. Because the moment we become institutionalized we're going to lose."

Coda: The Promised Land

"We need a movement; we're nowhere." After John Perdew said that to me, I tried testing the statement and reviewed the reasons why it may or may not be true. Both perspectives, I found, had an equal weight, and all I could do was say yes and no at the same time.

Today I can at least revise the claim, or half of it. We're not nowhere. If there is one thing my search turned up, that would be it. The forms of the movement, its basic structures, abide. Moral Monday is proof of that, and the Algebra Project, though it is important to remember the movement's core matter will always remain singular. I thought of that when driving around the Mississippi Delta with Jessie Tyler, on those choppy gravel roads washed out by rain. It was easy, in that setting, to get back to square one. Away from the schools, or the marches and sit-ins and bullhorns and police—away from anything that looked like the rest of America to me—I was reminded that the movement, by definition a mass, still depends on personal volition, on individual virtue and decision. And it's hard, I thought, really hard. A commitment to the common good can come at quite a cost. Being unable to help so many in need of care, Tyler told me, was causing her to exhibit post-traumatic symptoms.

At first I was afraid to tell people what my book was about. Announcing the project, I would brace for a torrent of reproof or dismissal, even charges of heresy. *How dare you compare that time with our own, you weren't there, you don't know*: I imagined all these responses. Yet almost invariably I encountered the opposite, and while that sounds consoling, it was not always. When telling those I met I thought the civil rights movement was still among us, or could be, I could sense how easily that vision merged with their desire. People want the movement to be alive, very much so, and I know why: it changes the story. If the lesson of Selma and Greensboro is that anything can be done, and then, in the standard telling, all that promise and energy runs out, then it really is tragic, it really is the saddest story—unless the movement does go on, in which case we don't know how it ends.

At times I was the only one willing to argue against my thesis. Just because it is convenient for it to be alive, I would say, doesn't make it so. But such resistance was never marshaled with any conviction on my end; it was only a device used in debate, to see what might be stirred in reply, though I already knew the strongest reply: history, not desire, makes it so. The search as carried out in this book is by no means complete or exhaustive. The list of people and organizations I might have visited in addition to those I already have is long. But more important than the number of profiles or interviews was to make sure my travels fell along a fairly wide gamut. So I sought out the young and old as well as those in between, and aggregates ranging from the NAACP, with its long history and large membership, to the Dream Defenders, whose existence is in the earliest and most inchoate stages. Stretching the book along such a span, I hoped, would provide structure to a search that could be limitless in size.

If the civil rights movement counts as a tradition, I now believe it is one that can be characterized by invention above all else. I recall a conversation I had with a professor, a historian of education. He knew of the citizenship class on Johns Island and had written his dissertation on the freedom schools of the Summer Project. He was young and white and had been greeted with some hostility for taking on subjects normally seen as belonging to African

Americans. But that's where the best examples of creativity were to be found, he told me; in order to study communities taxed by circumstance and devising novel methods, he had no choice but to turn to the history of black schools.

Jonel Edwards of the Dream Defenders had also turned to that history, and was thinking of ways, in the year 2014, of designing her own version of the citizenship schools. That idea, like others, survives the passing of generations, and there can be no better proof of its vitality. Many of the movement's techniques are like that; they appear invulnerable to age, though that is not to say there are no blind spots. The vote, education: they swirl around like an idée fixe, drawing attention away from other concerns. "One great fault of the movement," Julian Bond said to me, "is that even though it has always touched on economic themes, it has not fought as strongly for economic justice as it ought to have, in my view. We in the movement have been derelict in raising these economic concerns and having them at the forefront."

When Perdew said we need a movement, he was talking, of course, about the broad sweep, about demonstrations on the scale witnessed fifty years ago. Continuum means constancy of being though not necessarily of intensity, which can wax or wane along the way. And in that respect I believed Perdew was also talking about himself. A Coloradoan, a student at an Ivy League college, he volunteered for SNCC and ran the gauntlet, was jailed in Albany and Americus but decided to stay. It is important to know, in other words, that if, as Moses said, the country is going to assemble in a larger sense, then many will have to be present who on the face of it have no obvious reason for enlisting. The sit-ins, Moses is on record as saying, woke him up, compelled him to go South, and events of that time also brought Perdew down, and Howard Kirschenbaum from Johns Hopkins. When is this generation going to wake up, I have heard Moses ask, and it is a structural discontent, of course, for every generation is upset with its successors. Still, the question bothers young activists like Phillip Agnew, but was Moses talking about them, the Dream Defenders, or about another group, the millions of uninitiated, say? It is all of us, finally, who must be awakened.

And so the struggle continues. Will it ever end? The finish line David Dennis sees as a recurring illusion: "Prior to 1964," he said, "segregation sort of hit you in the face. You had separate rest-rooms, separate water fountains—everything was right there. After 1964, it wasn't, so people got this false sense of accomplishment, that feeling *we've made it*. You can compare that to the euphoria that passed over the black community when Obama was elected. We got a black president—okay, we have gotten there now."

The chain, he said, could stretch on into infinity—we're there now, or maybe *now*, and so on. "The nature of it," said Moses, "is a long-term, ongoing struggle, passed on through the generations; you find the passing on of what happened in the fifties to a generation that will spend their lives in the twenty-first century." Bob Zellner, his old McComb ally, was willing to go further. "We have reached the promised land, because we now know the promised land is the struggle itself," he told me. This remark was unforgettable, something I never heard anyone else say. I even asked if he would record it in my notebook, and here's what he wrote down: "'68—45 yrs. ago Dr. K said may not get there with you. Well we have gotten to the P.L. The P.L. is the struggle itself. We have a freedom song: 'freedom is a constant struggle.' Shakespeare—'the play's the thing.'"

"'The play's the thing'?" I asked in the restaurant, looking over his note.

"Yeah, the journey's the thing," he said, and mentioned Sisy-phus—"that guy who pushed the rock up the hill. It's an existential, philosophical proposition."

King, on his last night, the night of April 3, 1968, said: "We've got some difficult days ahead. But it really doesn't matter with me now, because I've been to the mountaintop. And I don't mind. Like anybody, I would like to live a long life—longevity has its place. But I'm not concerned about that now. I just want to do God's will. And He's allowed me to go up to the mountain. And I've looked over, and I've seen the promised land. I may not get there with you. But I want you to know tonight, that we, as a people will get to the promised land."

The speech was rousing, a total affirmation, and to watch it on YouTube is to be moved to the highest degree, to register the same sort of shudder or sense of dilation as at any authentic work of art. Zellner's words, on the other hand, seem to suggest toil, effort, and enervation, but it is also the opposite of that. It is a liberation in itself. I think of the euphoria of the freedom high, for instance. Suddenly you're in the right place and doing the right thing, so all those questions that normally must be batted away from conscious thought—why don't I stand up for what I believe in; why aren't I doing more?—are no longer there. The self, unmanacled in this way, feels much lighter.

"This shit is hard, man, every day," Agnew said to me when we were talking about the Dream Defenders' campaigns. "I've learned a lot about myself, my insecurities and my strengths, throughout, that I didn't really learn when I was safe and sound in a job. We have this relationship with race that is brooding. Everyone sees it and feels it and tastes it, but we can't talk about it; it makes people very uncomfortable, and taps into that place in your brain that is so subconscious. People don't realize they are having these thoughts or feelings until they have to choose a side, and that's what the conflict is about; that's what the catalyzing is about."

Race taps into that part of our brain that is unconscious, he said, and I thought of that when watching the news reports from Ferguson, Missouri, in November 2014, when a grand jury decided not to indict the police officer who fatally shot Michael Brown and the National Guard was called in to prevent a riot. The next week, a grand jury in New York refused to indict a cop who had arrested Eric Garner, an African American from Staten Island, and placed him in a chokehold. Video of the incident showed Garner saying "I can't breathe" over and over, and he died from a heart attack an hour later. In response to these events, protests sprang up in several cities, and for a time it seemed like everyone in America was talking about race. Though not always intelligently, it must be said. The vocabulary of racism, timeless in its narrow, thwarted articulation, filled the airwaves and social media. One encountered terms like "thugs" and "those people" without any accompanying regard for the connotation or lineage of such phrases; just as Agnew had said, it was the unconscious that was in control and doing the talking, and far too often the unconscious seemed to be nothing but a jumble of stereotype, denial, and herd mentality.

In those days Zellner's remark took on an additional weight or profundity, and I understood it anew, with original force. The struggle is the promised land: I took that to mean, at least in part, that maybe you can't change America, not always or not that much. America would go on being what it was—but your relationship to it could change. Zellner had chosen to try and move it, like Sisyphus pushing the boulder up the slope time and again, and he would be altered by the contest, even if nothing else was.

Moses used to consult existentialists such as Camus, the author of *The Myth of Sisyphus*, and at dramatic moments. "When I was in jail this last time," he said in the early months of 1964, "I read through *The Rebel* and *The Plague* again. The main essence of what he says is what I feel real close to—closest to. It's the importance to struggle, importance to recognize in the struggle certain humanitarian values, and to recognize that you have to struggle for people, in that sense, and at the same time, if it's possible, you try to eke out some corner of love or some glimpse of happiness within. And that's what I think more than anything else conquers the private bitterness."

As my search wore on, I asked most of my subjects for a definition of the promised land. Tyler outlined a traditional view when she said it was a place "where we are all treated as one," and I thought of her answer when Minor alluded to the decades ahead. "Slowly but surely," he said, "we're becoming a country where there's no majority. It's not going to be majority white, majority black or Hispanic. It's just going to be America." The preacher in him, though, was skeptical of the outcome, and he pointed me back to the original tale: "When the children of Israel got to the promised land, it was a continuous struggle. But the biggest struggle ended up being against themselves."

And Barber, another Southern preacher, told me, "King knew enough of the Bible to know that even when Joshua took the people into the promised land they still had to face Jericho. You have to understand victories of the past as partial victories. My father helped integrate schools, but it wasn't true integration. We got the right to vote but what we need is to get everybody who's eighteen automatically registered, like you are for war. We got a health care bill, but what we really need is health care for all, period. And that's why the struggle is a constant march, a constant mood."

So do you see Zellner's comment as a concession, I asked, an acknowledgment that you cannot win or hope to reach the promised land in this life?

"No, you're not conceding that you can't win. You're understanding that life is a struggle, sometimes to get out of bed. Evil is going to always be present; that's a reality, but not a morbid reality, because then the possibility of transformation is always present."

For this reason, he continued, you must engage in struggle if you want to live out the fullest meaning of your humanity. That meaning, one's gradual realization of it—thoughts like the ones that occurred to Moses in jail—is what balances out, I guess, all that is traded or lost along the way, for the civil rights movement exacts plenty, even as it holds out the promise of liberation. As

Barber and I were talking I remembered a comment by Franklin McCain, one of the four students who entered Woolworth's in Greensboro on February 1, 1960, to eat in the white-only section. "If it's possible to know what it means to have your soul cleansed," is how he described feeling when he sat down at the counter. On that day, he said, he felt better than he ever had in his life.

Acknowledgments

This book, or at least the germ of it, started one night in Petersburg, Virginia, when I had dinner with Nancy and David Dennis. Over sushi we discussed the Mississippi Summer Project and what they call "the fundamentals" of organizing. I was nervous about the meeting, and David later said, with a laugh, that he went along only because Nancy had given me a tentative endorsement. But the two soon became some of my closest and most essential friends, and I could not have written *In Search of the Movement* without their wit, hospitality and candor.

A week in Petersburg gave me the idea of writing a book; as vague and notional as that idea was—and its premise would evolve over the following year—I knew even then that I wanted City Lights to publish it, and the soundness of that instinct has been ratified many times over. I am blessed by the tact and acuity of my editor, Elaine Katzenberger. Stacey Lewis has been another indispensible ally, and I am grateful as well for the efforts of Chris Carosi, Linda Ronan, and Robert Sharrard.

Writing *In Search of the Movement* forced me to neglect from time to time the documentary I was producing. Dava Whisenant managed *The Blues House* whenever I needed a furlough, and it would be difficult to imagine a more sensitive or capable collaborator. I am also obliged to Sheila Griffin, who traveled to Greensboro one day to photograph the Woolworth's that was site of the February 1, 1960 sit-in. One of these images is featured on the book's cover.

Finally, of course, I would like to thank everyone who agreed to be interviewed. Not every conversation is included or mentioned in these pages, but that does not diminish the debt, and I want to cite in particular the testimony given by Marion Helland, Freeman Hrabowski, Jakki Jefferson, Jim Kates, Anne Littleton, Gerald Mackey, Gwendolyn Patton, William Saunders, and Sherika Shaw. Their reflections inform much of *In Search of the Movement* even when the credit is not made explicit. For introductions or their assistance in arranging interviews, thanks are due to Laurel Ashton, Sarah Bufkin, Shamile Louis, Benjamin Moynihan, and Charmeine Turner.

Notes

Unless otherwise noted, all quotes are from the author's interviews.

Introduction

"The nation couldn't deny": *Quality Education as a Constitutional Right*, 83

"One way to think about": talk delivered by Robert Moses at South Carolina State University, April 9, 2014

"It appeared that": "Almost a Riot," Louisville *Courier-Journal*, October 31, 1870, 4

"Returning at later point in time": *Collected Essays*, 567

Part One

1.

"Desegregation prove itself": A facsimile of the notes Parks took during the sessions at the Highlander Folk School is available at the Civil Rights Movement Veterans website: www.crmvet.org/docs/5507park.htm

"Mrs. Parks, this is the case": *My Soul Is Rested*, 43

"If we are wrong": *The Autobiography of Martin Luther King*, 60

2.

"classical period": Bayard Rustin, "From Protest to Politics: The Future of the Civil Rights Movement," *Commentary*, February 1, 1965, www.commentarymagazine.com/article/from-protest-to-politics-the-future-of-the-civil-rights-movement/

"A demonstration": *Who Speaks for the Negro?*, 239

"The final thing that civil disobedience does": "The Man Behind Moral Mondays," *The American Prospect*, June 17, 2013. http://prospect.org/article/man-behind-moral-mondays

3.

"There is no doubt": The *Shelby v. Holder* opinion can be accessed via the Supreme Court's website: www.supremecourt.gov/opinions/12pdf/12-96_6k47.pdf

"In The Court's view": Ibid.

"no one's vote": "Justice Department to sue North Carolina over voting law," *Washington Post*, September 30, 2013. www.washington-post.com/politics/justice-department-to-sue-north-carolina-over-voting-law/2013/09/29/123cbbce-292d-11e3-8ade-a1f23cda135e_story.html

"The North Carolina measure": "NC Senate approves GOP-backed election changes," Election Law Blog, July 25, 2013, http://electionlawblog.org/?p=53461

"As the weeks passed": *Walking with the Wind*, 69

"Today, much of our activism": "Interview with James Lawson," *The Believer*, March/April 2013, 74

"We are now involved in a serious revolution": *Walking with the Wind*, 219

"Freedom is not enough": Quoted in *Freedom Is Not Enough*, ix

Part Two

1.

"virtual slaves": *Refuse to Stand Silently By*, 15

"Often in the starlit evening": *Army Life in a Black Regiment*, 125

"it was the Johns Island folk": *Echo In My Soul*, 52

"That made a lasting": Quoted in *Freedom's Teacher*, 96

"I never married again": *Refuse to Stand Silently By*, 20

"with the exception of the NAACP": *Freedom's Teacher*, 184

"I was surprised": Quoted in *Freedom's Teacher*, 222

"This is not going to happen": *Refuse to Stand Silently By*, 248

"I knew that there was a lot of illiteracy": Ibid.

"too juvenile": Ibid., 251

"I can never explain": Ibid., 252–253

"I had her teach the session": Undated affidavit by Bernice Robinson, Bernice Robinson Papers, Avery Research Center, College of Charleston, Box 3, Folder 8

"The citizenship schools are for adults": *Echo In My Soul*, 201

"The purpose of this amendment": Bernice Robinson Papers, Box 3, Folder 16

"We weren't interested": Quoted in *Freedom's Teacher*, 274

"We wanted to make": *If Your Back's Not Bent*, 129

"more than 50,000": *Freedom's Teacher*, 302–303

"The classes had not changed": *I've Got the Light of Freedom*, 166

2.

"To me, social justice": *Echo In My Soul*, 236

"*Parting the Waters* is dedicated": *The King Years: Historic Moments in the Civil Rights Movement*, 2

"Like anybody": *The Autobiography of Martin Luther King*, 365

"King stood still for once": *At Canaan's Edge*, 766

"Wherever they are assembled today": *The Autobiography of Martin Luther King*, 360

Part Three

1.

"I have said repeatedly": "Feds Reject Mississippi's Plan for Insurance Exchange," NPR.org, February 8, 2013, www.npr.org/blogs/health/2013/02/08/171485790/feds-reject-mississippis-plan-for-insurance-exchange

"In such an environment": *The Good Doctors*, 230

"The comprehensive": Ibid., 229

"Is there a meaningful": "Text of Rustin Call for Rally in Support of Poor," *New York Times*, June 3, 1968, 49

"If the governor": "North Carolina Republicans put Ideology Above Lives," *Washington* Post, July 28, 2014, www.washingtonpost.com/opinions/dana-milbank-north-carolina-republicans-put-ideology-above-lives/2014/07/28/724081cc-169e-11e4-85b6-c1451e622637_story.html

"They don't want": Ibid.

2.

"The sit-ins hit me powerfully": *Radical Equations*, 3

"He wasn't distracted": *I've Got The Light of Freedom*, 106

"better known as COFO": David Dennis, interview for *Eyes on the Prize*, November 10, 1985. Accessed digitally: http://digital.wustl.edu/cgi/t/text/text idx?c=eop;cc=eop;rgn=main;view=text;idno=den0015.0245.025 148:

"complicating all this": "SNCC at Fifty," *The Root*, April 15, 2010. Accessed digitally.

"From now on": *Pillar of Fire*, 590

"I saw three distinct groupings": *Radical Equations*, 96

"Poor Bob": Ibid., vii

"When I left Mississippi": Alexis Jetter, "Mississippi Learning," *New York Times* Magazine, February 21, 1993

"He is more or less": *Letters from Mississippi*, 19

"In the Algebra Project": *Radical Equations*, 119

"the root function": *Notes of a Native Son*, 170

"Our national policy": Talk delivered by Robert Moses at College of Charleston, April 10, 2014

"he thinks that the whole school system": *Who Speaks for the Negro*, 92

"In today's world": *Radical Equations*, 5

"the question remains": Ibid., 12

"They didn't have": Jetter, "Mississippi Learning"

3.

"butting their heads": quoted in *The Good Doctors*, 29

"Many people felt": David Dennis, Memo to National Action Committee Accessed via Civil Rights Movement Veterans website: www.crmvet.org/docs/63_core_dennis_nac-r.pdf

"I always thought": *The New Abolitionists*, 189

"You're in an organizing mode": *Radical Equations*, 182

"In order for us": *Radical Equations*, 3

4.

"We are a movement": "Sitting In to Fight 'Stand Your Ground,'" *New York Times*, August 12, 2013, A10.

Coda: The Promised Land

"We've got some difficult days": *The Autobiography of Martin Luther King*, 365

"When I was in jail": *Who Speaks for the Negro?*, 95

"If it's possible to know": *My Soul is Rested*, 78

List of Works Cited in Notes

Baldwin, James. *Notes of a Native Son*. Beacon, 2012.

Branch, Taylor. *Pillar of Fire*. Simon and Schuster, 1998.

_____. *At Canaan's Edge*. Simon and Schuster, 2006.

_____. *The King Years: Historic Moments in the Civil Rights Struggle*. Simon and Schuster, 2013.

Carson, Clayborn, ed. *The Autobiography of Martin Luther King*. Warner Books, 2001.

Charron, Katherine Mellon. *Freedom's Teacher: The Life of Septima Clark*. University of North Carolina Press, 2009.

Clark, Septima. *Echo In My Soul*. E.P. Dutton, 1962.

Cotton, Dorothy. *If Your Back's Not Bent: The Role of the Citizenship Education Program in the Civil Rights Movement*. Atria, 2012.

Dittmer, John. *The Good Doctors*. Bloomsbury, 2009.

Ellison, Ralph. *Collected Essays*. Modern Library, 2003.

Higginson, Thomas Wentworth. *Army Life in a Black Regiment*. Dover, 2002.

Lewis, John. *Walking with the Wind*. Simon and Schuster, 1998.

Martínez, Elizabeth, ed. *Letters from Mississippi*. Zephyr Press, 2007.

Moses, Robert. *Radical Equations*. Beacon, 2001.

Patterson, James T. *Freedom Is Not Enough*. Basic Books, 2010.

Payne, Charles. *I've Got the Light of Freedom: The Mississippi Organizing Tradition*. The University of California Press, 1995.

Perry, Theresa and Robert Moses et al., eds. *Quality Education as a Constitutional Right*. Beacon, 2010.

Raines, Howell. *My Soul Is Rested: The Story of the Civil Rights Movement in the Deep South*. Penguin, 1983.

Warren, Robert Penn. *Who Speaks for the Negro?* Vintage, 1965.

Wigginton, Eliot, ed. *Refuse To Stand Silently By*. Doubleday, 1992.

Zinn, Howard. *SNCC: The New Abolitionists*. Haymarket, 2013.

ABOUT THE AUTHOR

Benjamin Hedin has written for *The New Yorker, Slate, The Nation, The Oxford American,* and *The Chicago Tribune.* He is the editor of *Studio A: The Bob Dylan Reader,* and has taught at New York University and the New School. Hedin is also the producer and author of a forthcoming documentary film, *The Blues House.* www.benjaminhedin.com